C000291620

When FOOTBALL Was FOOTBALL

EVERTON

© Haynes Publishing, 2011

The right of Michael Heatley to be identified as the author of this Work has been asserted
by him in accordance with the Copyright, Designs & Patents Act 1988.

All rights reserved. No part of this publication may be reproduced, stored in a retrieval system
or transmitted, in any form or by any means, electronic, mechanical, photocopying, recording
or otherwise, without prior permission in writing from the publisher.

First published in 2011

A catalogue record for this book is available from the British Library

ISBN: 978-0-857330-46-8

Published by Haynes Publishing, Sparkford, Yeovil,
Somerset BA22 7JJ, UK
Tel: 01963 442030 Fax: 01963 440001
Int. tel: +44 1963 442030 Int. fax: +44 1963 440001
E-mail: sales@haynes.co.uk
Website: www.haynes.co.uk

Haynes North America Inc., 861 Lawrence Drive,
Newbury Park, California 91320, USA

Images © Mirrorpix

Creative Director: Kevin Gardner
Designed for Haynes by BrainWave

Printed and bound in the US

When FOOTBALL *Was* FOOTBALL

EVERTON

A Nostalgic Look at a Century of the Club

Michael Heatley

Contents

Introduction

History may count for precious little in an era where clubs name their new stadia after their sponsors and while players and managers alike hop on board a gravy train unleashed by Sky and the Premier League that shows little sign of slowing. If it did, then Everton – founder members of the Football League, ever-present in the aforementioned Premier League and proud residents at Goodison Park for the majority of their existence – would surely run away with the honours every season.

True, a younger, less historic outfit across Stanley Park has enjoyed a modicum of success over the years and even, every so often, left the blue half of Merseyside in the shade. But when it comes to the crunch, Evertonians are as loyal and tenacious as the heroes – from Jack Sharp through Dixie Dean and Alan Ball to Ratcliffe, Latchford, Southall and Sheedy – who have carved out their club's history.

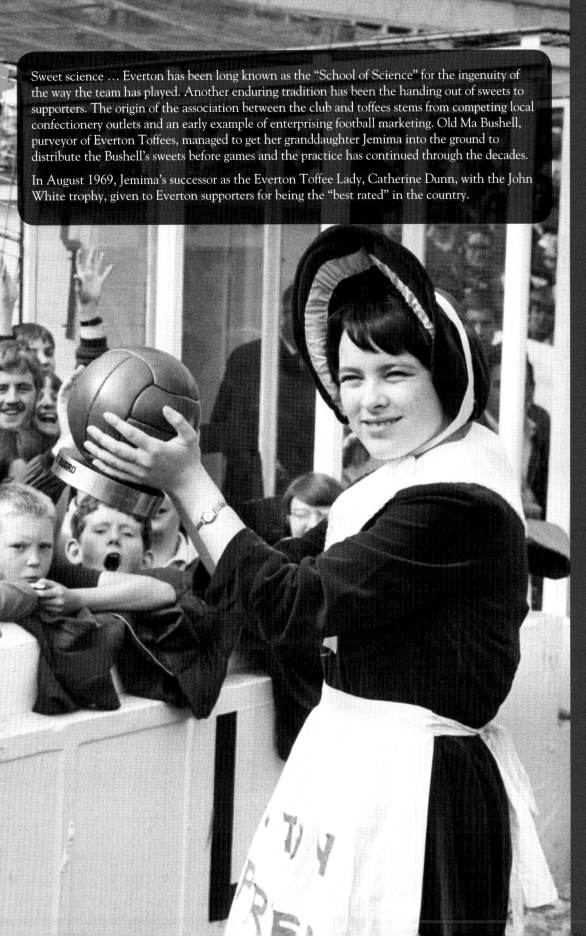

Sweet science … Everton has been long known as the "School of Science" for the ingenuity of the way the team has played. Another enduring tradition has been the handing out of sweets to supporters. The origin of the association between the club and toffees stems from competing local confectionery outlets and an early example of enterprising football marketing. Old Ma Bushell, purveyor of Everton Toffees, managed to get her granddaughter Jemima into the ground to distribute the Bushell's sweets before games and the practice has continued through the decades.

In August 1969, Jemima's successor as the Everton Toffee Lady, Catherine Dunn, with the John White trophy, given to Everton supporters for being the "best rated" in the country.

Few would trade any amount of silverware for the thrill they feel as the hair-raising *Z Cars* theme blasts out from the Goodison tannoy and the boys in blue take to the field for another hard-fought game.

When Football Was Football: Everton rolls back the years, recounting the triumphs and, yes, sometimes disasters that have made following Everton such an entertaining experience. The pictorial material from the *Daily Mirror* archives has been supplemented by reproductions of some of the paper's sports pages from years gone by, adding a definitive "I was there" feeling that will put you on the terraces, blue scarf and rattle in your hand and rosette proudly on your chest, as the likes of Kendall, Ball and Harvey bossed the midfield, and flamboyant goalkeeper Gordon West held the Gwladys Street End in the palm of his hand.

The book covers Everton in Europe, in Cup finals, on open-top buses with trophies and even, briefly, in the Second Division. No matter how many ups and downs the club has undergone in the past, it has remained in the top flight now for several decades and thankfully seems set to remain there.

Whether you're a new fan interested in catching up on history and folklore or an old stager taking a trip down memory lane, there's something for everyone between these covers, celebrating one of the nation's truly great clubs.

Domingo to Dean
1865-1939

The 1933 FA Cup final at Wembley. Everton's great goalscorer Dixie Dean is pictured in action against Manchester City. Dean scored once in a resounding 3-0 victory.

The early history of Everton Football Club, as with so many of their early contemporaries, is entwined with church and cricket. It was in the district of Everton, which became part of the city of Liverpool in 1835, that the English Methodist congregation New Connexion was formed by Guto Sion Jones in 1865. Three years later the church made the decision to build a new chapel, buying land on Breckfield Road North between St Domingo Vale and St Domingo Grove. St Domingo Methodist Church was duly opened in 1871, taking its name from a building built in 1758 by West Indies trader and future Mayor of Liverpool George Campbell, who had spent much of his working life in the colony of Santo Domingo. In 1877 the Reverend Ben Swift Chambers formed a cricket club. It quickly became apparent that the boys wanted to keep playing sport throughout the year and, as cricket was a summer sport, they opted to form a football club to occupy the winter months. Thus, in 1879, St Domingo's FC was formed. Interest in the football club soon expanded beyond the church and in November the decision was taken to change the name to Everton Football Club in order to reflect the area. The new club was one of the founder members of the Football League in 1888 and, two years later, were league runners-up; 1891 saw Everton become league champions for the first time, setting in train a period of sustained success over the next four decades and establishing the club as one of the biggest in the country. Bitter disputes with landlord and local MP John Houlding led to a move away from Anfield to a new stadium called Goodison Park in 1892 (and the formation of Liverpool AFC). Further success for the city's first club was to prove frustratingly elusive as Everton finished as frequent runners-up in both league and cup from 1893, until victory in the FA Cup in 1906. Everton were again victorious in the 1914–15 league campaign, but would have to wait until the arrival in 1925

RIGHT: The 1897 Everton FA Cup final team that lost 3-2 to Aston Villa at the Crystal Palace. Everton's goals came from Jack Bell and Dickie Boyle, and they actually led 2-1 after half an hour, but could not stop Villa winning and completing the cup part of a famous Double. All five goals came in the first half.

of Dixie Dean for another burst of trophy-winning success, beginning with the league title in 1928, followed by a brief period of relegation to the Second Division and then another top-flight title in 1932. A second FA Cup followed a year later, before the club's fifth league title in 1939.

Dangerous Scots forward Jimmy Dunn is foiled by keeper Langford during an Everton raid on the Manchester City goal, September 1933.

> *Behold Goodison Park! … Taking it altogether, it appears to be one of the finest and most complete grounds in the kingdom.*
>
> – Out of Doors, 1892

Everton grew up in the environment of working-class streets common to many football clubs. The rows of terraced housing surrounding the ground helped give the stadium its character as well as being the source of much of its support. In 1965 the old houses on Goodison Avenue were due to be demolished to make room for a new stand.

In 1888 Everton were involved in the meetings and subsequent decision to launch the Football League. A crowd of 12,000, more than double than anticipated and easily the biggest of the day, saw Everton beat Accrington 2-1 at Anfield on 8th September. They would finish the season in eighth position, a good 20 points behind the Invincibles of Preston, but quickly settled into league football.

They won their first league title two years later, but left their Anfield home when landlord John Houlding raised the annual rent by 150 per cent. Everton moved across Stanley Park in 1892 and Goodison Park hosted its first match on 1st September, a friendly against Bolton Wanderers. Liverpool joined the Football League in 1893 and won promotion to the top flight at the first attempt, setting up a local rivalry that continues to this day. Everton won their first meeting and at the end of the season were runners-up, while Liverpool were relegated.

The century ended with Everton having just a solitary league title to show for their efforts. The new century promised much, with a new secretary-manager in Will Cuff and the club finishing runners-up in the league in 1902, 1905, 1909 and 1912, even if the top spot still eluded them.

LEFT: The greed of Anfield landlord John Houlding led to Everton's departure in 1892.

Everton's new ground, Goodison Park, remains their home today in spite of plans to move to a new £400 million development in Kirkby.

THIS ROAD
IS PRIVATE

GOODISON
AVENUE 4

UNADOPTED

SNAPSHOTS OF WEEK·END FOOTBALL

(1) Some of the 40,000 crowd at Birmingham watching Everton beat Liverpool in the Cup semi-final. (2, 3, and 4) At Stoke Woolwich Arsenal were put out of the Cup final by Newcastle United; photographs show Woolwich shooting at goal, a fight for the ball, and Aitken centring. In the Everton v. Liverpool match at Birmingham: (5) Balmer (Everton) breaking up the forward line; (6) Scott (Everton) saves with a punch; and (7) Scott, in mid-air, after running out of goal to save. (8) Old Carthusians beating Old Reptonians at Queen's Club in the Arthur Dunn Cup final.

A crowd of 50,000 travelled down from Merseyside to Villa Park in 1906 to witness Everton's semi-final victory against their old adversaries and Merseyside neighbours; they won comfortably 2-0 to book their place in the final.

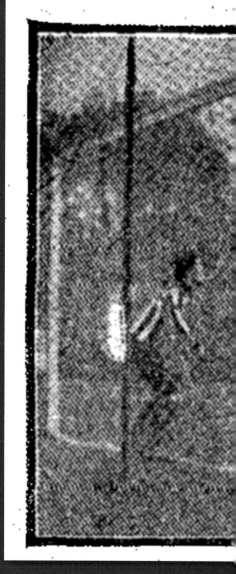

EVERTON

There was consolation in the FA Cup in 1906, where Everton, having reached the final and lost in 1893 and 1897, would eventually make it third time lucky in the competition. They were to meet Newcastle United in the final at Crystal Palace, a ground where Newcastle had had no luck whatsoever during the decade. So it proved on the day: Sandy Young claimed the only goal of the game to earn Everton their first triumph in the competition (below). They reached the final the following season too, although this time Sheffield Wednesday scored four minutes from time to seal a 2-1 victory.

Typical photograph of football partisans' eager intensity in watching their favourite players.

EFEAT NEWCASTLE AT THE PALACE.

Dixie Blues

By the time Everton kicked off the 1914–15 season Britain was at war with Germany. While many felt football should be all but abandoned while the country was at war, others saw the normality of playing league fixtures as being good for morale. Irrespective of the rights and wrongs of either argument, it was a season that would at last see Everton cross the line ahead of their rivals, finishing a point ahead of Oldham at the end of the season to lift the league title for only the second time in their history. They were to hold on to the trophy for longer than expected, league football being halted until the 1919–20 season because of the ongoing First World War.

By the time normal football resumed, the side that had won the league title had all but gone and Will Cuff had stepped down (eventually becoming chairman) to be replaced by Tom McIntosh. Everton were not alone in losing many fine players to the hostilities but they seemed to take longer than most to recover. While Liverpool would win back-to-back league titles and Huddersfield go one better with their three in a row, Everton languished in mid-table for much of the decade. There was to be one exception, the 1927–28 season.

For much of the campaign interest had focused on Huddersfield, who were leading a two-pronged assault on both the League and FA Cups, with Everton merely at the head of a pack of clubs trying to catch them. But, in the shape of a young Merseysider who had made the trip across the great river from Tranmere, the Toffees had a formidable weapon...

LEFT: Visiting Spanish forward Zamora visits Goodison Park in 1931 and is introduced to the local hero, Bill Dean.

–LEGENDS–

Dixie Dean

William Ralph Dean, universally known as "Dixie", owes his place in Everton and football history to a record established in just one season, 1927–28. Dean scored a record-breaking 60 goals for Everton in the First Division, reaching the landmark with a hat-trick on the final day of the campaign. It is unlikely this will ever be beaten.

Dean began his professional career at Tranmere Rovers in 1923, where he showed early signs of ability by scoring 27 goals in 30 appearances for the club. Two years later he moved to Everton for a fee of £3,000. In his first full season as an Evertonian he scored 32 league goals, six short of the league record, but Dean was then involved in a motorcycle crash, breaking his jaw and fracturing his skull. Doctors told him he would never play again, but just 15 weeks later he defied their prediction and returned in a reserve game.

Dean went on to smash records, scoring a phenomenal 60 goals in a single season in 1927–28, thus playing a pivotal part in Everton's league triumph that year. Not surprisingly, such success caught the eye of the England selectors, and Dean scored twice during his international debut against Wales in 1927. Two goals against Scotland at Hampden Park on his second appearance ended a 23-year run of Scottish dominance over England on home soil. He won 16 caps in total and scored an incredible 18 goals, including hat-tricks against Belgium and Luxembourg.

After a magnificent career at Goodison that ended when he lost his place in 1937 he went on to play briefly for Notts County and Sligo Rovers in Ireland. Dixie Dean died, aged 73, in March 1980, after watching his beloved Everton play Liverpool at Goodison. A statue was erected at the ground as a permanent memorial in 2001.

William Ralph "Dixie" Dean in action for Everton in April 1937, shortly before he left the club after 13 years of exemplary service.

FOOTBALL
–STATS–
Dixie Dean

Name: William Ralph Dean

Born: Birkenhead, 1907

Died: 1980

Position: Striker

Everton Playing Career: 1925–37

Club Appearances: 433

Goals: 383

International Appearances: 16

Goals: 18

" *When I was playing I couldn't afford a pair of boots never mind boutiques.* "

Dixie Dean to George Best

Dean pictured during a training session at Goodison Park in April 1933. He had joined the club in 1925 from Tranmere after being spotted by Tom McIntosh and had netted 32 goals in his first full season.

Dean was replaced in 1937 by the equally prolific Tommy Lawton, but the general consensus was that manager Theo Kelly had let Dean go too early and that, with Dean and Lawton in tandem, Everton would have been unstoppable.

As Dean continued rattling in the goals during the 1927–28 season, so Everton caught up with Huddersfield. Where Huddersfield would let both points slip with a defeat, Everton would collect one with a draw. A seemingly unassailable lead was pulled back; at the beginning of April Huddersfield held a five-point lead over Everton (and were through to the FA Cup final) with eight games left to play. Eight points was considered enough to lift the title, but only if Everton won all their remaining matches. Everton rose to the occasion and kept winning while Huddersfield all but collapsed, with Everton heading the table for the first time a week before the season came to a close.

Going into the penultimate match Dean was on 53 goals for the season – a four-goal haul in the 5-3 win over Burnley at Turf Moor kept Everton at the top, a point ahead of Huddersfield and with one match left to play, while their rivals still had three games left. In what proved to be a disastrous month for Huddersfield, they would collect only five points from the eight league matches and let the league slip away before losing in the FA Cup final. Indeed, Everton were crowned champions without having to play after Huddersfield crashed to another defeat, so on the final day of the season attention turned from the race for league honours and onto Dixie Dean's personal quest for glory.

With barely eight minutes left, an Alec Troup corner floated invitingly into the Arsenal penalty area and Dean rose above all to head home his 60th of the season. Even an Arsenal equalizer with barely seconds left could not dampen the enthusiasm of the Goodison crowd.

LEFT: Dixie Dean in 1930. Everton were relegated to the Second Division that year, but Dean stayed with them as they won promotion in 1931, followed by the First Division again in 1932 and the FA Cup in 1933 (he scored in the final itself) – an unprecedented three-year sequence of success.

RIGHT: The *Mirror* reports on the remarkable title race won by Everton.

WEDNESDAY NEARLY SAFE

Point Gained at Highbury Brings Spurs Nearer Relegation

EVERTON CHAMPIONS

A dramatic goal in the last half-minute of their match with Arsenal at Highbury enabled Sheffield Wednesday to draw an exciting match and to get very near to League safety.

They still want one point, and have the chance of getting that from their home match with Aston Villa on Saturday, to ensure absolute safety: meanwhile, as the subjoined table of present positions shows the Spurs will be very fortunate indeed if they escape relegation:

	P.	W.	D.	L.	F.	Agst.	Pts.
Tottenham Hotspur	42	15	8	19	74	86	38
Sheffield Wednesday	41	12	13	16	79	78	37
Middlesbrough	41	11	15	15	81	85	37
Sunderland	41	14	9	18	71	76	37
Manchester United	41	15	7	19	66	79	37

Sunderland play Middlesbrough at Middlesbrough on Saturday; Manchester United are at home to Liverpool, and the Spurs have finished their campaign. Not until Saturday night will the descending clubs be known, but it looks very much as if the North London club will be one of the unhappy pair because of their poor goal average.

Wednesday were more impressive than the Arsenal in the first half last night, but the Gunners lasted better, and with a quarter of an hour to go Brain headed a goal for them. Wednesday fought back superbly and Arsenal were lucky more than once before Seed headed in the equaliser.

Huddersfield lost their championship chance when they lost to Aston Villa last night, Walker, Dorrell and Waring scoring for the Birmingham men without reply. Everton are assured of the championship whatever happens on Saturday.

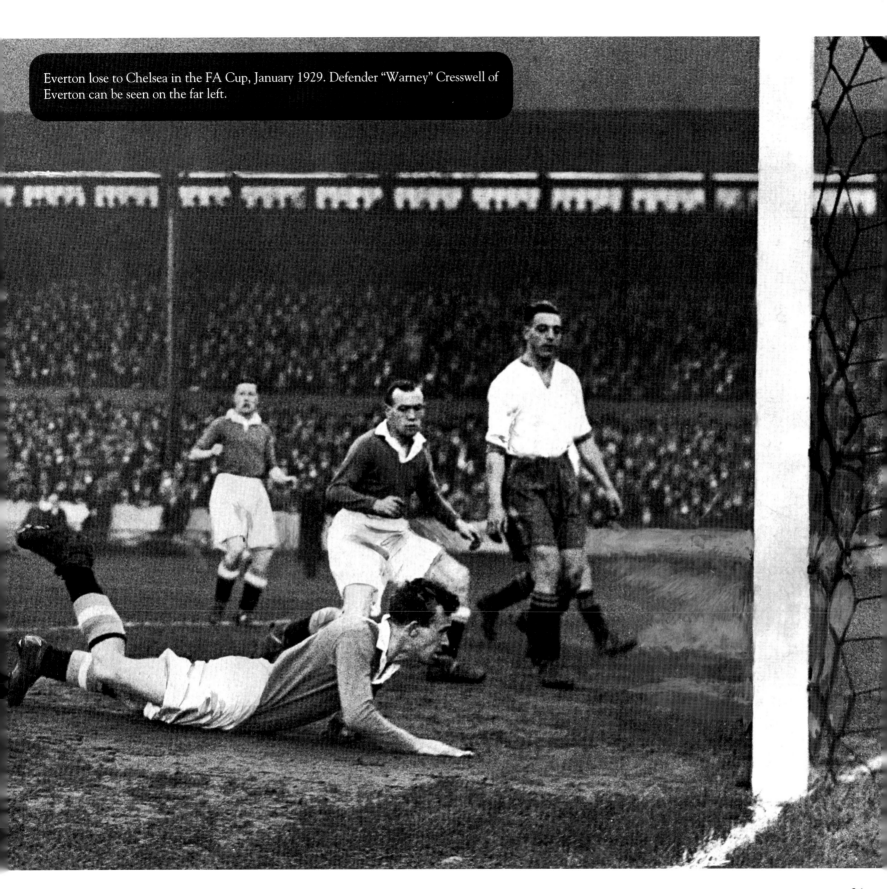

Everton lose to Chelsea in the FA Cup, January 1929. Defender "Warney" Cresswell of Everton can be seen on the far left.

TO-DAY'S LEAGUE GAMES

Clubs in Relegation Zone Fighting for Points

EVERTON FOLK ANGRY

Although the League is a secondary matter compared with the Cup semi-finals, some interesting games of great consequence to clubs concerned in the fight against relegation are to be played.

Grimsby Town, at the very foot of the league ladder, are to entertain Burnley, a side that is reasonably but not yet absolutely safe. Grimsby seem certain to be relegated.

Everton, who are in deplorable position for a club with such a tradition, are not engaged, but their supporters are, it is reported, very angry because Dixie Dean, once the greatest goalgetter of his time, has been chosen to play for their reserves to-day.

V. Gibbins.

A northern correspondent says, " the supporters are incensed and say it is a shame that such a man should be risked against Birmingham Reserves." Newcastle, another club with a splendid history, have also fallen on evil times. They are to welcome Manchester City to St. James's Park. Newcastle are on the upgrade while the City are faltering, so that the Tynesiders may be able to get the points that lead to League safety.

While Sunderland were constantly changing their team they lost matches. For the last four weeks they have been represented by the same side and have turned the corner. It will, however, be surprising if they win to-day at Leicester.

At home to Bolton Wanderers, Birmingham are anxious to avenge the home defeat they sustained in the corresponding game last season, and they should about realise their aim, although they will be without Haywood.

VILLA IN FORM

Aston Villa, who are doing splendidly now, are due at Anfield, where they will find that Liverpool have also reached their best form. Mandley continues at outside-right for the Villa in place of York.

Vivian Gibbins returns to the West Ham team that is to oppose Leeds. The corresponding game last season produced ten goals, eight of them counting for the Hammers.

Such a score is improbable to-day, but the points are likely to remain in the keeping of the East End club.

Derby County may be back at the top of the table to-night. They have to visit Sheffield United at Bramall-lane, and the Blades will be strengthened by the return of Green.

It will be necessary for Portsmouth to call on Rutherford again to-day, as Cook is still on the injured list. It looks as if the naval town side will concede both points to the Rovers at Blackburn.

Fall and Rise

The *Daily Mirror* (left) tells the sad tale of Everton's decline and fall into the Second Division – relegated from the top flight for the first time in their history.

Scaling the league summit had been a difficult task, but one Everton had achieved in spectacular fashion – and this makes their almost immediate collapse all the more difficult to fathom. After finishing champions in 1928 Everton fell to 18th the following campaign, and worse was to follow. At the end of the 1929–30 season Everton found themselves at the wrong end of the table. This collapse came despite having much the same nucleus of players who, two years earlier, had won the title!

Fortunately Everton's sojourn in the second tier lasted only 12 months. They topped the table by seven points and scored 121 goals to earn an immediate return to the First Division.

If losing had become a bad habit between 1928 and 1930, then winning so often and so well in 1930–31 became a good habit the following campaign as Everton returned to the top flight and finished the season two points clear at the top.

Cup Finalists Both Score Good Friday Wins

WEDNESDAY'S LATE GOAL

Everton are making as sure as they can of the League championship. Their defeat of West Bromwich Albion was quite the outstanding feature of yesterday's football.

What should have been a splendid game at Goodison was largely spoilt by the introduction of too many fouls.

The game was also once held up from a very unusual cause, some of the players being bothered by the string from a loose kite which flew over the ground.

Dean, who was in capital form, scored in the first half from a pass by Dunn. Late in the game W. G. Richardson equalised, but Dunn proved his quality by adding the winning point for the home side.

Arsenal were forced to play second fiddle to Derby County for some time, but eventually Lambert put the Londoners in front from a pass by Hulme, and added another following a blunder by Collins. Bowers eluded the close watch of Roberts to reduce the County's arrears.

LEICESTER'S GOOD FIGHT

Newcastle, the other Cup finalists, just scraped home against Leicester. The City twice took the lead in a hard match through Lochhead and Chandler, but Newcastle netted through Starling, Allen and Boyd.

Sunderland and the Villa shared the points, but the home team were fortunate, and the Villa protested strongly against the goal the Roker men were credited with.

Chelsea were full value for their victory over Bolton Wanderers at Stamford Bridge. Gallacher got the first goal and then Jackson got two beauties to clinch matters.

Sheffield Wednesday beat West Ham by a last-minute goal at Upton Park. Ruffell put the Londoners in front, but Rimmer headed an equaliser, and then when a draw seemed inevitable Ball beat Hufton rather easily.

Grimsby, scoring through Hobnes and Dyson, beat Middlesbrough in Bestall's benefit match, but Blackpool, Grimsby's companions in misfortune, had to be content with a draw on their own ground against Portsmouth.

EVERTON A STEP NEARER THE CHAMPIONSHIP

Chased for much of the time by reigning champions Arsenal, Everton once again ground out results when it mattered in the 1931–32 season. Equally impressive was their goalscoring, which saw them top the 100 mark once again, netting 116 goals on their way to their fourth league title.

As one of the best teams in the land during the 1930s, Everton was modestly represented in the national side. The England team of 1938 featured two Everton players, Joe Mercer (fifth from left, back row) and Tommy Lawton (centre front).

While Everton could not retain league consistency going into the 1932–33 season they still ended the campaign with silverware, marching all the way to Wembley in the FA Cup final. Their opponents were Manchester City, whose light blue shirts were deemed to clash with Everton's stripe. In an unprecedented move the FA instructed both sides to change colours on the day, with one to be allocated red and the other white. Luckily for Everton, the white shirts were awarded to them on the toss of a coin.

The shirts were also numbered in a final for the first time, with Everton wearing 1 to 11 and Manchester City 12 to 22. White proved to be something of a lucky charm for Everton, who ran out 3-0 winners thanks to goals from Jimmy Stein, Dixie Dean and James Dunn.

RIGHT: Dixie Dean holds the FA Cup trophy after Everton's victory over Manchester City.

REFEREE IN AFTER-THE-CUP COMEDY

Walks Off with Ball
Geldard Secured

PLAYER WINS!

Congratulations for Dixie Dean as he left the royal stand with the famous Cup.

BY OUR OWN CORRESPONDENT

It seems that no Cup Final can pass without an "incident" of some sort, but that which occurred at Wembley on Saturday must be without parallel.

The final whistle sounded and there was a concerted rush for the ball by the players. Geldard, the Everton winger, got to it first. He picked it up, grinning broadly, and tucked it under his arm.

Then, to the amazement of the great crowd, the referee—Mr. E. Wood—walked over to Geldard and appeared to demand that the ball be handed over to him.

Geldard demurred, but Mr. Wood was insistent, and for a few moments both men had hold of the ball, although there was no suggestion of a struggle.

Player Wins After All

Finally Geldard delivered up his treasured souvenir and lined up with his victorious team-mates in readiness to receive the Cup and the medals.

Apparently the matter was settled later in the dressing-rooms, for when the teams had changed it was seen that Geldard had regained the ball.

The attendance at this Cup Final, in which Everton beat Manchester City by 3—0, was 92,950, as against 92,298 in 1932.

Despite the fact that it was announced some time ago that all seats were sold, there were at least 2,000 people walking about outside the enclosure, hoping to get in.

For the first time in the history of the Cup the players were numbered, and it was agreed that this was a great help to the spectators.

To-Night's Welcome

Everton played in white and Manchester City in red.

Before the match the teams were presented to the Duke of York and afterwards received the Cup and medals from the Duchess.

Everton celebrated their victory in the evening with a dinner and dance at an hotel, where they were given a rapturous welcome by supporters. Their rivals held their own little jamboree in another hotel.

When the Everton players return home to-night they will parade Liverpool in the four-in-hand which carried the team to victory when they last won the Cup in 1906.

When the final whistle went, Geldard, the Everton outside right, secured the ball. Mr. Wood, the referee, made him give it up and left the field with it; but later, when Everton left the Stadium, it was seen that Geldard had again secured the coveted trophy.

ABOVE: The *Daily Mirror* tells the tale of an epic Cup final win in 1933. There seems to have been some controversy about the whereabouts of the match ball. Albert Geldard was one of several flying wingers Everton had in the period, others being Torry Gillick, Wally Boyes and Jimmy Caskie.

RIGHT: Goalkeeper Ted Sagar, one of the key Evertonians of an era that promised so much but did not quite deliver. Everton could and should have built on the 1933 FA Cup triumph, but a succession of events conspired against them. Tom McIntosh died from cancer in October 1935 and was replaced by club secretary Theo Kelly. Seen as a remote, autocratic and petty figure by many of the players, Kelly would preside over the break-up of the once great side and bring in replacements not quite up to the standards of their predecessors.

Everton's final League Championship of the decade, in 1938–39, is often seen as happening despite, rather than because of, Theo Kelly. Indeed, Kelly was not given the official rank of manager until after the title was won, the Blues finishing four points ahead of Wolverhampton Wanderers. Once again, war brought normal league football to a halt with, however, Everton as the champions. It would be six years before another ball was kicked in anger.

–LEGENDS–

Ted Sagar

Ted Sagar clocked up 24 years and one month as a player at Goodison Park, a spell interrupted by the war years of 1939 to 1945 yet nevertheless unlikely to be rivalled. And Sagar's spell as custodian – he was stopping them at one end when Dixie Dean was scoring at the other – meant he ruled from Thirties to Fifties.

Doncaster-born Sagar was snatched from under the nose of Hull City and brought to Goodison as he turned 20. His first season saw the club finish bottom of the First Division, but he missed only one game as they bounced back the following year. Only four England caps arrived to recognize his exemplary club record, though the likes of Vic Woodley and Harry Hibbs were formidable rivals for the national number one shirt.

On the club front, the league titles of 1932 and 1939 plus an FA Cup win in 1933 were rewards for his efforts. The Championship season saw him miss just one game, and that was lost 7-0, underlining his importance to the team. The physically unimpressive Sagar used anticipation to beat burly centre-forwards, outjumping them and deftly evading their physical challenges.

As the Fifties approached Sagar found himself alternating in goal with George Burnett, who had been his wartime replacement. Instead of moving on, he hung up his gloves at the end of the 1952–53 season, having played 463 league games and 32 FA Cup ties.

Ted Sagar died in 1986 and did not live to see Neville Southall beat his league appearance record. Nevertheless his place in Everton folklore is assured.

Ted Sagar in action during the Second Division match at the Dell against Southampton, August 1951.

FOOTBALL
–STATS–

Ted Sagar

Name: Edward Sagar

Born: Moorends, 1910

Died: 1986

Position: Goalkeeper

Everton Playing Career: 1930–52

Club Appearances: 497

Goals: 0

International Appearances: 4

Goals: 0

The legendary, long-serving Ted Sagar in training. He joined Everton at the age of 20 and left in his mid-forties. His last appearance at Plymouth made him the oldest player to represent the club.

"One Happy Family" Put Us There

Mr. Theo Kelly
(Everton F.C.)

WITH Everton requiring only one point at Charlton to-day to make certain of the League championship, we asked Secretary Theo Kelly for the secret of his club's success.

Here's his reply: "The word 'happiness' may look soft in print, but believe me that's our secret, **and a very essential factor in** successful football it is," he said.

"Have a cheery, contented team, an atmosphere free of petty jealousies and quarrels, and officials who are fair-minded and encouraging" (this with a laugh) "and you will have a club half-way to the top of the League.

"**Skill without co-operation and team-spirit is practically wasted.**

Anyway, all the boys have been grand this season, and have worked and played like Trojans, so I think I can say without boasting that we deserve our successes."

And so say all of us.

♦   ♦   ♦

At four o'clock this morning nineteen-year-old William Hindmarsh, amateur footballer will go to the pit with his pals as he has done many times before.

Somewhere around mid-day he will leave his work, hoping that this will be the last time he makes that journey.

Then, his pit boots and clothes laid aside he will set out for Sunderland, ready to take his place in the gallant Willington team which meets Bishop Auckland in the Amateur Cup final.

A couple of hours later, whether his team have won or lost, William will bid farewell to the other side of this man's make-up. When those who do know of it talk of him, they speak not of the brilliance of the Molineux chief, but of the pluckiest struggle they ever saw, a fight he made to conceal his pain from his friends.

Loyalty to his club has prevented him from joining a League club before. Three times he has turned down offers of £6 a week although he earns only 25s. at the pit.

"I promised to stay with Willington as long as they were in the Cup," said William.

And he has kept that promise. So when the

JOHN THOMPSON'S SPORTFOLIOS

cheers of the crowd have died down. William will become a Portsmouth player.

Thousands of Soccer fans throughout the country know Major Buckley of the Wolves as the manager who has sold £120,000 worth of footballers and has now guided his club to the Cup Final and a distinguished position in the League.

That is the man who is justly famous to-day, his moves discussed everywhere, his achievements coming from a strange mixture of daring and shrewdness. . . . Undoubtedly a man of ideas in a game which has need of such show-men.

Because he won't talk about it himself, few know of the other side of this man's make-up. When those who do know of it talk of him, they speak not of the brilliance of the Molineux chief, but of the pluckiest struggle they ever saw, a fight he made to conceal his pain from his friends.

Let Mr. C. B. L. Prior, for twenty years a Norwich City director, tell you about that scene.

"Difficult team problems preceded our match with Crystal Palace in September, 1919, and the decision of Major Buckley, who was then our manager, to turn out relieved some of our

manager changed. Major Buckley was putting on a brave front, but we could see that all was not well.

"Eventually he sorrowfully admitted it would have to be his last game. By the time we reached Liverpool-street he was becoming very distressed.

"**I can picture him now, fighting not to let us see how ill he was, and one side of the compartment was cleared for him to lie down.**

"Long before we reached Norwich we were very alarmed. Afterwards at his home we awaited news from the doctor, and he was very grave.

"It was the same great courage he showed on the field which helped Major Buckley to pull through the anxious days that followed. . ."

This, then, is the man who will proudly watch his team battle against Portsmouth before the King and Queen at Wembley next Saturday . . . I think you will agree he has earned his reward.

♦   ♦   ♦

Stone of sausages to be shared out among the boys . . . just for being good lads. That's the reward an admirer has sent Luton's players.

The admirer is a Southend man, who was

anxiety when we boarded the train at Norwich," he said.

"He always was a well-developed robust player, and playing centre half used every ounce of energy."

It was as a centre half that Major Buckley achieved pre-war fame with Villa, Birmingham and Derby.

How great was the risk he took in playing for Norwich on that day no one knew until later. He had been seriously wounded on the Somme in the previous year, a wound from which he had not then fully recovered.

"He was obviously determined to enthuse the depleted side with the will to beat bad luck," added Mr. Prior.

"His was an exhibition of tremendous pluck."

The late Mr. Eric Fulcher, a fellow director and close friend of the Major, was with us when we discussed the game while the delighted with the gentlemanly behaviour of the team when they visited his establishment recently.

He promised that if they won at Chesterfield he would give each of them a pound of sausages.

♦   ♦   ♦

Arsenal are keeping their usual close watch on the north-east for likely youths.

Manager Allison is taking an interest in William Blakemore, centre half of Deaf Hill Juniors, who soon will be seventeen. He stands 6ft. and is of strong build.

Partly because of the colour of his hair, his height and his style of play, young Blakemore has been named locally as a second "Ginger" Hill. In his schooldays he played for Durham County schoolboys. His head work is said to be particularly good.

The Right Blend

Blend of experience and youth has given Ashford F.C., members of the Kent League, one of their most successful seasons ever.

On Thursday, April 27, they meet Bexleyheath and Welling in the final of the Kent League Cup on Charlton's ground, and are also challenging Northfleet for the League championship.

A semi-professional side, the players include painters, a tyre-maker, plasterer, sawmill labourer, gymnastic instructor and railway factory workers.

Much of their success is due to the brilliant displays of centre forward Reg Tricker, old Arsenal and Clapton Orient favourite, who has scored forty goals to date. Other ex-League players are Pickett, former Queen's Park Rangers goalkeeper, Todd, once of Airdrieonians, and Hogarth, West Ham.

Last year Newgate-street won promotion in the Hertford and District League. This year they have lost twelve, drawn one and won but two of their fifteen matches. But they say they don't mind much if they are relegated again, because there have been so many withdrawals from the First Division that a club only gets a match every two or three weeks.

"**We don't mind what division we are in, as long as we get our game every Saturday,**" says Secretary Bayly.

Newgate-street's president is Mr. A. Menzies Sharpe. The club are not on gland treatment!

Proved Worth

While some clubs persist in spending fortunes to buy success, Tottenham Hotspur, pioneers of the "nursery" system, still pin their faith in the youngsters.

I hear that five of the young men at Northfleet, having proved their worth, will be moving to White Hart-lane when the season ends.

Three of them are English lads, one Welsh and the other a Scot.

Twenty-one-year-old Norman Evans, a left half, has already distinguished himself by gaining an amateur international cap. At White Hart-lane he joins friend Ronnie Burgess, who played with him in the same village team in Wales.

Ronnie has been earning good opinions for his displays at right half in the first team. It will be a great day for these lads if they appear together in a League match.

The other lads are: Edwin Ditchburn, goalkeeper, found almost on Northfleet's doorstep; Sidney Lown, nineteen-year-old Newcastle-born centre half; Leslie Bennett, an inside right, from Wood Green, London, and Roddie McLean, centre half from Clacknacuddin, a small Scottish village.

Everton's success was ascribed by Theo Kelly to a "family feeling". It was said, however, that the senior players like Joe Mercer and Ted Sagar worked out the tactics in training between themselves and came up with a side and formation that was good enough to win the league – with or without Kelly at the helm.

Two legendary Everton players, Joe Mercer (left) and Tommy Lawton, played together at Hampden Park for England against Scotland in April 1939. Both would remain with Everton until the war's end, though official football was suspended for the duration.

Tommy Lawton's all-round popularity transcended club loyalties. Indeed, it was such that his image was used to sell breakfast cereal, rather like Ian Botham in a more recent age.

FOOTBALL
–STATS–

Tommy Lawton

Name: Thomas Lawton

Born: Farnworth, 1919

Died: 1996

Position: Forward

Everton Playing Career: 1936–39

Club Appearances: 95

Goals: 70

International Appearances: 23

Goals: 22

On his death in 1996, *The Independent* newspaper described Tommy Lawton as "the princeliest, the most complete, simply the best centre-forward in Britain as the 20th century approached its half-way mark". Perhaps the reason he didn't become more of a legend was his habit of flitting from club to club; being rebellious by nature, he would rarely outstay his welcome.

Signing from his first club, Burnley, at the age of 17 for a £6,500 fee, a record for a teenager, Lawton played his first Goodison season alongside the soon-to-depart Dixie Dean, learning much from the legendary marksman. He readily took on Dean's mantle, his 28 goals in 1937–38 the highest in the First Division, though Everton only finished in 14th place. Lawton was still just 18 years of age.

The following season he hit 35, helping the Toffees secure the Championship and earning himself a full England call-up though still in his teens. England would play eight internationals before the outbreak of war, with Lawton playing in all of them. He scored in the first six, equalling a record for goals in consecutive internationals.

In the 1939–40 season he scored in the first two games. The possibilities were boundless, but war intervened, football was abandoned and Lawton served in the army as a physical training instructor. He also guested for Greenock Morton and for Chester, scoring five times in a match against a Royal Air Force XI in May 1943. He scored 152 goals in 114 games during the conflict, and netted 24 times in 23 wartime internationals.

On the advent of peace Lawton fell out with Everton and, after scoring 70 goals in 95 appearances, was transferred to Chelsea. The Toffees made a £4,000 profit on the deal, but had peacetime football been possible it's likely Lawton would have created even more of a legend for himself in Everton history. As it was he flitted from club to club before enjoying an Indian summer, age 34, at Highbury.

His 231 goals in 390 league games, and his 22 strikes in 23 internationals, were only the tip of the iceberg; *The Independent*, again, called him "one of the finest footballers Britain has produced", and few who saw him would disagree.

In later life Lawton would comprise one of the wise men on the pools panel. Here he is, alongside Tom Finney, when the panel was convened during the big freeze of 1963.

Smells like team spirit … As the 1930s and the first chapter of the Everton story drew to a close, Jimmy Cunliffe (left) and Billy Cook shared a post-training bath. They played for a club that ranked as one of the giants of the British game: its foundations were built on a bedrock of committed support in the heart of Liverpool, topped off with an honours haul of seven major trophies.

Back to the Top
1946-1960

A new postwar age for football and Everton, but amid the fresh faces are some more familiar ones. Training in 1953 are (left to right): Cummins, Sagar, Grant, Fielding, Cross, Leyland, Potts, Donovan, Moore and McNamara.

Having won the league title in 1939, Everton held the trophy for seven years, but it was to be nearly 20 more before the club tasted league success again. The departures of Tommy Lawton and Joe Mercer seemed to embody the reduced circumstances of the club. No aspect of life in Britain was left unaffected by the Second World War. Goodison Park itself was hit by a German bomb in 1940 that caused considerable damage to the Gwladys Street Stand, with repairs costing some £5,000 being paid for by the War Damage Commission. As peace finally resumed, the team was still a huge draw, confirmed by a record Goodison crowd of 78,299 in the match against Liverpool in 1948, but this was an extended period of decline and only modest recovery. The Board showed ambition with the then record £20,000 signing of Harry Potts from Burnley in 1950 but form suffered and the team were relegated in 1951, a 6-0 thrashing from Sheffield Wednesday confirming the Toffees' second and, to date, last relegation in the club's history. Manager Cliff Britton who had taken over from Theo Kelly steered the side to an FA Cup semi-final in 1953 and promotion a year later. Britton made way for Ian Buchan in 1956 as Everton consolidated their First Division status on the pitch – and made substantial progress under it thanks to the installation of undersoil heating in 1958, the first such facility in the world. Arguably the biggest development in the club's history during this period was the arrival of John Moores onto the Board in 1960. The former head of Littlewoods provided the funding for signings such as Jimmy Gabriel, Roy Vernon, and the £40,000 purchase of Alex Young from Hearts. Young, the man dubbed the "Golden Vision", would play a central part in the broadening horizons of Everton.

Everton's Jimmy Corbett (right) attempts to stop the mercurial Len Shackleton of Sunderland from getting his shot in as the Toffees visit Roker Park, 1948.

By October 1950 Dixie Dean had swapped scoring goals for pulling pints. In a familiar scene of "ex-player runs pub", the club legend showed off his England caps behind the bar of the Dublin Packet in Chester.

"
I know you've come here to take my place. Anything I can do to help you I will. I promise, anything at all.

Dean to his successor, Tommy Lawton
"

Everton's postwar years were not happy ones. The ground had been repaired, but of far greater impact was the loss of several players through injury and age.

To add to this, there was the falling out of Joe Mercer and Theo Kelly, with Kelly claiming the player had not tried during an international match. Mercer had sustained a serious cartilage injury, confirmed by an orthopaedic consultant, but the Everton manager refused to believe him and Mercer had to pay for surgery himself. To have treated any player in such a manner would have been unacceptable; to do so to a professional as dedicated as Joe Mercer defied belief.

In late 1946 the player was sold to Arsenal, with Kelly so keen to get him out of the club he brought Mercer's boots to the transfer negotiations so Joe would not have a reason to return. Joe would have the last laugh, however, collecting a runners-up medal in the FA Cup and winning the league title with Arsenal before hanging up his boots for good in 1955.

Tommy Lawton also departed the club for Chelsea and Kelly tried to sell star defender Tommy "TE" Jones to AS Roma for £15,000, this deal being thwarted by foreign currency regulations rather than footballing matters! Having inherited a hugely talented squad, Theo Kelly had almost single-handedly dismantled it and failed to replace the players like for like.

His tenure finally came to an end in September 1948, with the club having finished no higher than 10th in the league since the war. He was replaced by former Everton player Cliff Britton, a former member of the 1933 FA Cup-winning side, although the chalice he was now handed had undoubtedly been poisoned.

The official Everton 1950 team photo. Back row (left to right): T Falder, "TE" Jones, T Sagar, J O'Neill, G Burnett, P Farrell, C Lello, M Lindley. Middle row: O Hold, Ted Buckle, E Wainwright, H Catterick, T Eglington, W Fielding, J Grant. Front row: J W Parker, E Moore, A Hampson, J Humphreys, G Saunders, T Clinton.

Everton's loss in the guise of Joe Mercer was Arsenal's gain.

SHOOT TO 'KILL' IS THEIR FIRST AIM

TRIO OF FAVOURITES

WAINWRIGHT   FALDER   FARRELL
Three of Everton's most popular players, they played a big part in keeping the club in the First Division last season.

MORE fire in the attack is the policy at Goodison Park for Everton this season. Two years ago flaxen-haired Cliff Britton left Burnley to manage the club with whom he won an F.A. Cup medal in 1933, and immediately put into operation a defence-tightening policy. It worked.

Everton climbed to safety from the bottom of the First Division table. Last season the defence again warded off relegation.

Now the Goodison Park forwards come in for the Britton pep-up. They failed to score in sixteen League games last season.

Down at Bellefield, the club's training ground, I saw Wally Fielding, Eddie Wainwright, Tommy Eglinton, and Ted Buckle getting the range on the home-made Britton-devised shooting gallery, which Cliff hopes will mean all the difference between goals and those shots which only bring "Ooo's" from the crowds.

His idea to put Everton back among the goals and the points is a dwarf, full-width goal with the middle boarded up to leave gaps of some 3ft. at either end.

Everton's forwards are going to make goalkeepers bend this season. Bull's-eye goals on this training aid are turf-trimming shots which whip into the net just inside the posts.

BUT this is only part of the Britton plan. Heading tennis he considers to be one of the finest methods of tuning up the players; and equal importance is attached to dribbling, tackling, physical culture and track work in spikes.

Still Cliff is not a satisfied manager. He will not be until Everton are champions and have won the Cup again. The close season has seen Billy Higgins go to South America and Jack Hedley, a Bogota disappointed full back,

● As the League teams get ready for the big kick-off on August 19, " Daily Mirror " Soccer reporters, led by JOHN THOMPSON, are touring the clubs bringing you the latest news on their prospects. To-day JOE HUMPHREYS reports on Everton.

transferred to Sunderland —while Cliff's five-year plan to rebuild Everton is only in its second year.

But, Cliff says: "I have some promising lads coming along who can fill the gaps."

THE club's coaching scheme for fostering and encouraging youth is being stepped up.

Twice weekly these lads will go to Bellefield Training School, where one of the finest panels of coaches in the country will see them and put them on the stepping stones to Soccer stardom.

"Our aim," says Cliff, " is to keep the boys in their age groups and try to instil in them the basic points of the game in a progressive form of training. Any 'natural' ability they have we will endeavour to develop, not stifle."

And while Everton's accent is on youth, the club is not forgetting its old servants, and thirteen of them are to benefit by cheques this season.

Everton were active in the transfer market in the postwar period and fans were eager for news of acquisitions that would assist in the drive back to the top.

43

The league decline continued with a new man at the helm, with Everton finishing in 18th position in 1949 and 1950, although some respite came during the latter season when the club reached the FA Cup semi-final. Their reward was a clash with Liverpool at Maine Road, but, lacking a proven goalscorer in their ranks, their domination of the game came to nothing and Liverpool scored twice to book their place at Wembley. The disappointment heaped further pressure on Cliff Britton.

LEFT: Policemen at Maine Road, Manchester, await the arrival of the fans for the Merseyside derby Cup semi-final, 1950.

BELOW: Everton players in training with trainer Harry Cooke (far right). Players are (left to right): Leyland, O'Neill, Easthope, Parker, Hickson, Sutherland, McNamara and Harris.

CORRECT MONEY READY

The complete opposite to his predecessor, Britton was seen as approachable and easy-going. This did not mean he could be taken advantage of, however, for he was also a teetotaller and something of a disciplinarian. While he did much to raise confidence he could do little to improve results as the club slid even further down the league. Eleven consecutive defeats between September and November 1950 saw Everton at the wrong end of the table and they fell into the Second Division for only the second time in their history.

B C D E F G H J

Everton welcome lowly opposition Notts County to Goodison in 1952, one of the years when they were in exile from the top flight.

The hope within the club was that they would emulate their 1930s' predecessors and secure an immediate return to the top flight. The reality was entirely different. Incoming players such as Harry Potts and Jock Lindsay, and home-grown stars such as Dave Hickson and John Willie Parker, found it difficult to adapt to the rigours of Second Division football and the team was only able to finish seventh in its first campaign, a good seven points away from the promotion places. It got worse, too, with the 1952–53 season seeing the club fall even further down the table to their lowest ever position of 16th, only five points away from the embarrassment of relegation into the third tier.

Having halted a potential freefall, Everton began the 1953–54 season determined to bounce back. Hickson and Parker were to form a particularly lethal partnership. By the time the campaign came to a close at the end of April, the pair had scored 55 league goals between them, more than 50 per cent of the total that Everton scored in the campaign.

The season began encouragingly, with Everton seldom out of the top two or three during the opening months as they traded blows with Leicester City, Blackburn Rovers and Nottingham Forest. Inexplicably, however, they suffered something of a collapse as the end came in sight. After a 2-2 draw at Leicester City on 20th March, Everton lost at home to mid-table West Ham United (2-1) and away to Leeds United (3-1), were held at home by Stoke City (1-1) and similarly had to settle for a single point at both Fulham and Lincoln City over the Easter period, although they did take both points at home against Lincoln on Good Friday.

The Everton team of March 1953. Back row (left to right): Clinton, O'Neill, Lindsay. Middle row: Harry Cook (trainer), Fielding, Farrell, Jones, Lello, Potts, Cliff Britton (manager). Front row: Buckie, Cummins, Hickson, Parker, Eglington.

The *Mirror* sports pages at Easter reflected the uncertainty as stuttering Everton attempted to stumble over the line with the Second Division title.

By the time of the final full weekend's fixtures, Blackburn Rovers led the table with 55 points, Leicester City were second with 54 points and Everton were third with 52. However, Leicester and Blackburn were scheduled to meet and Everton, at home to Birmingham City, would have one final match away at Oldham Athletic in midweek. The clash between the top two at Filbert Street saw the home side run out 4-0 winners and put them at the top of the table, assured of promotion. A somewhat nervous Everton display in front of a phenomenal 62,865 fans at Goodison Park saw Dave Hickson grab the only goal of the game and bring them to within a point of Blackburn Rovers.

With Oldham having already been relegated to the Third Division North, the result of the final match at Boundary Park was never really in question. Such was the closeness at the top of the table, however, that a 6-0 victory or better for Everton would see them claim the Second Division title while a draw could see them missing out on promotion altogether on goal average! After the previous month's stuttering progress, it was a confident Everton that set about making the most of their second chance, with Parker (two), Hickson and "TE" Jones establishing an unassailable 4-0 lead by half-time.

They were unable to grab the two additional goals that would have won the title, but since the mission at the start of the day was victory and therefore promotion at all costs there wasn't too much disappointment at the final outcome. Besides, Liverpool's relegation from the First Division at the end of the same season meant Everton were once again top dogs in the city.

49

Top Flight Frustration

Everton play Charlton at the Valley in the mid-Fifties. It was a period when the club was content to tread water, rarely threatening to challenge for honours and content to be back in the top flight – especially as Liverpool were not.

Blackpool's immortal Stanley Matthews gives Everton full-back Dan Donovan a torrid time at Goodison, November 1954.

For the rest of the 1950s, promotion would prove to be the highlight. Seldom troubled by relegation and never threatening to mount a challenge on the title, the club spent almost five seasons in mid-table mediocrity. While Cliff Britton had hoped the Everton Board would use promotion as a springboard for further success and sanction big-name signings to bolster his squad, he was to be disappointed. Indeed, the Board appeared to go out of their way to drive a wedge between themselves and their manager, trying to appoint an acting manager while he was out of the country with the team.

Britton, however, proved to be the architect of his own eventual downfall, dropping and subsequently selling talisman Dave Hickson to Aston Villa for £17,500 in 1955. Eventually he could stand the Board's interference no more and handed in his resignation in February 1956, stating: "I want all managers to have the freedom to do the job for which they are appointed."

Everton players training at Goodison Park in preparation for an FA Cup match against the old enemy, Liverpool, in January 1955. Note the familiar Goodison landmark of the church of St Luke the Evangelist, and the absence of floodlight pylons. The latter would appear two years later.

Sharing a laugh as they go through their paces are (left to right): Moore, Jones, Lello, Fielding, Wainwright, Parker, Hickson, Eglington, Farrell, O'Neill, Rankin and Potts.

53

Jimmy Harris heads for goal and nearly scores against
Huddersfield Town but the ball comes back off the bar.
Everton won the game 5-2 in November 1955.

A slightly pensive Wally "Nobby" Fielding, pictured in 1956. Dubbed "Everton's favourite cockney", he played 410 times for the Toffees and contributed 54 goals to the cause over a 12-year Goodison career.

Dave Hickson challenges Fulham centre-half Brice in typically robust fashion, in April 1954.

FOOTBALL
-STATS-
Dave Hickson

Name: David Hickson

Born: Ellesmere Port, 1929

Position: Striker

Everton Playing Career: 1948–55, 1957–59

Club Appearances: 243

Goals: 111

International Appearances: 0

Goals: 0

-LEGENDS-

Dave Hickson

Centre-forward Dave Hickson enlivened a dour decade for Everton fans. His matinee-idol looks and fearless playing style made him the undisputed favourite of Goodison Park. Blues boss Cliff Britton spotted him playing non-league football for Ellesmere Port and signed him in 1948, but National Service halted his progress. He made his first-team debut in September 1951 and never looked back.

The same could not be said for the club, which was enjoying a rare spell outside the top flight. Hickson helped Everton finish second-tier runners-up in 1953–54 but he enjoyed only one more top-flight season before being sold to Aston Villa. Hickson had enjoyed a strike partnership with John Willie Parker and, while using his height as an aerial threat, he also had a powerful shot that earned him the nickname of the "Cannonball Kid".

His best moment came in 1952–53's FA Cup fifth round, where Second Division Everton beat Manchester United. Hickson scored the winning goal after returning bloodied to the field after a head injury.

Hickson returned via Huddersfield in 1957, the fee £10,000 lower than the previous £17,500 for which he was sold, but the goals failed to flow as before – he reached a total of 111 in 243 appearances – and he controversially moved on to Liverpool. His return of 21 goals in 27 games in his first season in red impressed new boss Bill Shankly, but after one more campaign he gave way, at 32, to younger men.

Hickson later went on to play for Tranmere Rovers, becoming the only footballer to have played for all three of Merseyside's professional clubs. But the fact he is employed by Everton as a guide on the popular stadium tours of Goodison Park suggests he remains a Blue. He also remained a keen player and would still turn out in charity games until well into his 60s.

–LEGENDS–

Tommy "TE" Jones

Thomas Edwin "TE" Jones made 411 appearances for the Blues between 1950 and 1961, having signed straight from school and turned professional on his 18th birthday in 1948. He had to wait six years before making his first-team debut and when it finally came he had to face Arsenal at Highbury.

A dependable defender, Jones followed in the footsteps of the legendary T G Jones who had been one of the club's star defenders in the Thirties and Forties. In fact "TE" began his first-team career as a full-back but moved over to take his namesake's place in the 1950–51 season. He proved to be a model of consistency in a disappointing decade.

He was part of the last Everton team to be relegated in 1951 and helped them gain promotion back to the top flight three years later. In 1957 he took over the captaincy, succeeding the departing Peter Farrell. He returned to left-back towards the end of his career, and was replaced at centre-half by a young Brian Labone. It was a source of disappointment to fans and the player himself that Jones never played international football, but he was part of the Football Association's team that toured Nigeria and Ghana in 1958.

A knee injury forced "TE" to retire at the age of 31 in 1961. After he hung up his boots Jones tried his hand at management and took charge of Toronto in Canada; he was only to stay one season but led them to a League and Cup Double. He then joined Littlewoods at the invitation of Everton chairman and owner John Moores, and was there for 30 years. He died in 2010 aged 80.

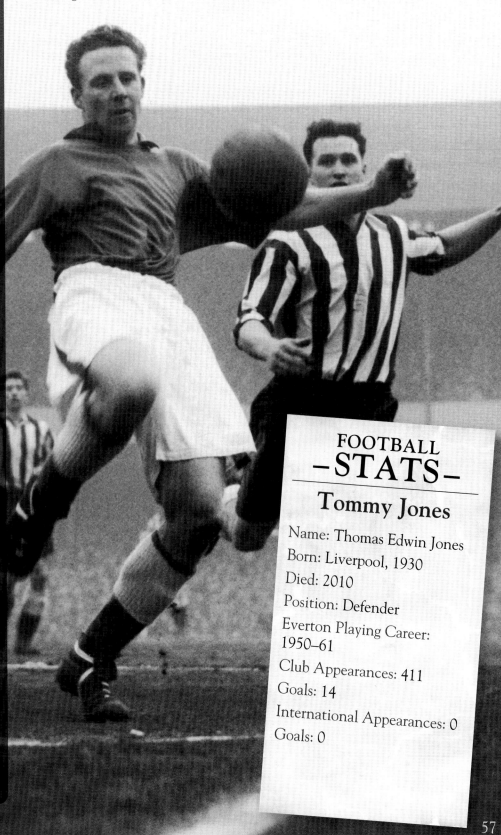

Tommy Jones of Everton gets the better of Newcastle centre-forward White during a match at Goodison in February 1955.

FOOTBALL –STATS–

Tommy Jones

Name: Thomas Edwin Jones
Born: Liverpool, 1930
Died: 2010
Position: Defender
Everton Playing Career: 1950–61
Club Appearances: 411
Goals: 14
International Appearances: 0
Goals: 0

57

Mirror SPORT
4 PAGES

Everton give a new job to an old servant

MANAGER? NO, HE'S THE FIRST A.O.(P.S.)

★ DIARY ★

GOLF.—Assistants' Tournament, Coombe Hill.

FOOTBALL.— Glasgow Charity Cup, 2nd round: Partick Thistle v. Queen's Park (7.0) at Hampden Park.

PUSKAS SEVERELY REBUKED

Ferenc Puskas, captain of the Hungarian football team, has been severely rebuked by the disciplinary committee of the Hungarian F.A. He was sent off the field during a league game in Budapest last month.

By GEORGE HARLEY

EVERTON directors have decided that they can manage without a manager.

They announced yesterday that Mr. Harold Pickering, 46, a club official, has been appointed Administrative Officer (Playing Staff) for next season.

He will work under the sub-committee of three directors who have been in charge of all playing matters since Cliff Britton, former England half-back, gave up the job of manager in February.

Whitehall Touch

Administrative Officer (Playing Staff), which sounds more like a job in Whitehall than at Goodison, is not a fancy title for manager.

Mr. Tom Nuttall, chairman of the sub-committee, made that clear yesterday when he said: " Mr. Pickering's appointment is indicative of our policy of not appointing a manager."

It is also indicative of the directors' belief that the club can get along quite well without former professional footballers in positions of control.

Mr. Pickering's association with big football has been purely administrative. He joined Everton's office staff thirty years ago, and has been in charge of the junior teams for many years.

Last week, Everton appointed Ian Buchan, 30, a Scot, as chief coach. He will have full control of the players' training.

Ex-amateur

Like the new Administrative Officer (Playing Staff), Buchan has never been a professional footballer.

A former schoolteacher, he played centre forward for Queen's Park, the only amateur club in the Scottish League, and was five times reserve for Scotland amateurs.

And nearly all the applicants beaten by Buchan for the job were former professional footballers.

The Everton experiment in club management will be watched with interest by other League clubs next season. But, whether it succeeds or fails, it is unlikely to start a new fashion in football administration.

The great managers— Matt Busby, Stan Cullis, Tom Whittaker, Jimmy Seed—were all professional footballers.

So were Alec Stock and Allenby Chilton, the men who took Leyton Orient and Grimsby respectively into the Second Division this season.

And the great majority of clubs will stick to the traditional idea that professionals are best equipped to manage professional clubs.

In the aftermath of Britton's departure, while Everton looked for someone to take the reins, a committee was convened to select the team. Eventually Ian Buchan was appointed chief coach, although for some reason he was never given the title of manager. Buchan set about improving the fitness of the players at his disposal, oversaw the return of Hickson after spells with Aston Villa and Huddersfield Town, and changed the style of play to fast, first-time passing reminiscent of Spurs' "push and run" style. But just as Spurs had discovered, the onset of winter and the heavier pitches it brought made it difficult for this style to work, and a run of six straight defeats saw Ian Buchan relieved of his position in October 1958.

ABOVE: The press try to make sense of the managerial mayhem going on at Goodison.

Excitement in a 1958 FA Cup tie at Roker Park as Everton striker Dave Hickson evades Hurley's outstretched leg to score the first goal. The game finished 2-2.

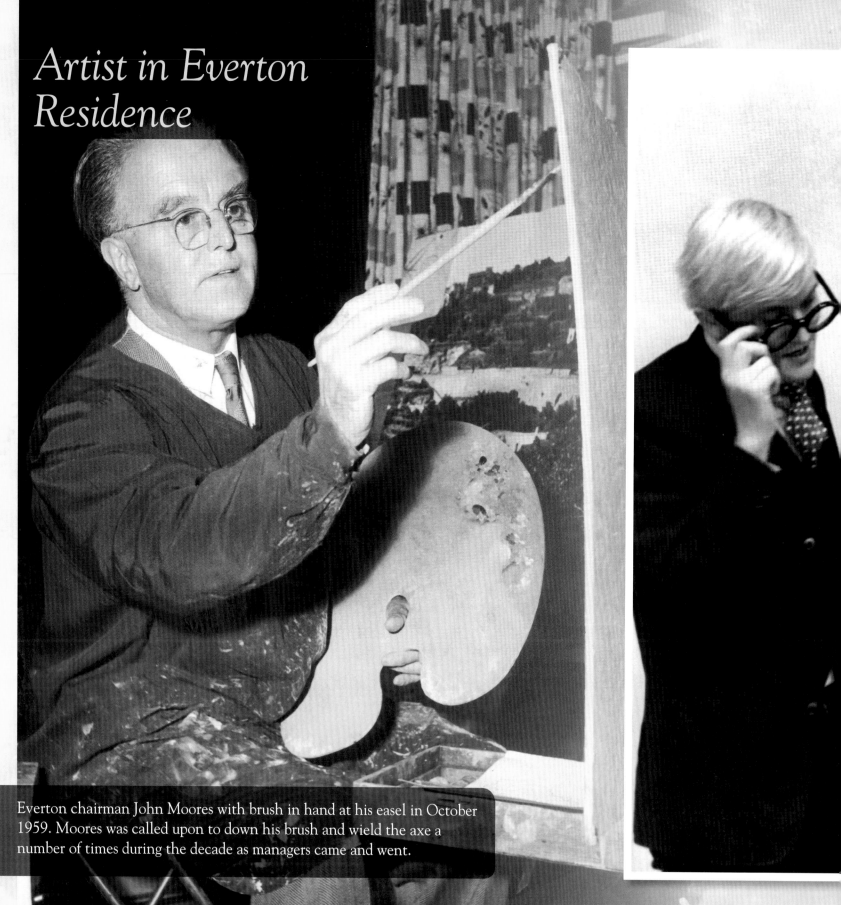

Artist in Everton Residence

Everton chairman John Moores with brush in hand at his easel in October 1959. Moores was called upon to down his brush and wield the axe a number of times during the decade as managers came and went.

Moores in conversation with David Hockney at Liverpool's Walker Art Gallery.

Everton in Action

Everton outside-right Jimmy Harris blasts the ball past
goalkeeper Bert Trautmann to score the first goal of a 3-1 win
against Manchester City at Maine Road, September 1958.

Everton goalkeeper Albert Dunlop caught in an acrobatic pose in November 1959. He played 231 league games between 1956 and 1963, the last a title-winning season.

FOOTBALL with FORWARD . . . The Man Who Knows Them All

EVERTON SEND SOS FOR CAREY

JOHNNY CAREY, shrewd Irish boss of Blackburn Rovers, is almost certain to become manager of Everton.

He was offered the vacant hot seat at Goodison Park yesterday. And I understand the offer is too good to refuse.

Everton's directors, who only two years ago declared that the term was out of date, have since seen their great club slump to the bottom of the First Division.

Now they have eaten their words by sending an SOS to Carey and offering him a salary of over £3,000 a house and a **FREE HAND** in running the club.

Carey told me after a meeting with the entire Everton board:

"I am not in the position to reveal any details of the offer. I must clear everything up at the Blackburn end before anything can possibly come from me."

● JOHNNY CAREY . . . £3,000-a-year and a house.

Offer is £3,000 a year and a 'free hand' as manager

SHAKEN

WHEN I broke the news to Mr. Norman Forbes, Blackburn chairman, he said:

"You have shaken me rigid—but I suppose this was really inevitable.

In fact, it's amazing that we have been able to keep Johnny Carey for so long, because he is undeniably one of the two best managers in the game.

"You can't keep a good man in little Blackburn.

"Johnny would be crazy to stay with us.

"We couldn't — and wouldn't — stand in his way."

NO CONTRACT

CAREY has been on a salary of £2,000 a year since becoming manager of Blackburn in 1932.

But he has never had a formal contract with the club.

A former Manchester

United and Eire right back, Carey steered Blackburn into the Second Division's top six in his first four seasons as manager.

Last season they won promotion, and reached the semi-final of the F.A. Cup.

This season they took the football world by storm, scoring five goals in each of their first three First Division fixtures.

STAR-HUNTS

TWO great talent hunts are under way. Object: To stop two great clubs staggering to the disaster of relegation.

BIRMINGHAM, struggling in the First Division, have sent out eight topline scouts with this instruction: "Report back the moment you find the men we need."

SUNDERLAND, the crisis club which has plunged to the foot of the Second Division, want at least three players just as urgently.

Birmingham manager Pat Beasley has joined his scouts touring the country.

And Mr. Harry Morris, chairman assures me:

"The money is ready and there will be no delay in buying as soon as we have found the right men."

NO CROWE

THEY hoped the first "Mr. Right" would be Chris Crowe, nineteen-year-old Leeds inside forward.

But Leeds turned down Birmingham's offer of a big fee plus winger Gordon Astall.

Sunderland's search—led by manager Alan Brown and southern scout Charlie Hewitt—is for a goalkeeper, full back, and inside forward.

Goalkeeper fancied is Peter Wakeham, of Torquay.

Last night Brown saw him play against Bradford, and sounded Torquay's directors about a transfer.

BAFFLED

DEREK TAPSCOTT, who set Ninian Park alight with his display on Saturday, is still baffled by his rapid move from Highbury to Cardiff.

He told me: "Two weeks ago I was informed by Arsenal manager George that he did not want to lose me.

"He said my chance would come again. Then, right out of the blue, he said I had no future with Arsenal, and Cardiff wanted me."

But Derek is happy now.

His tremendous performance in the 4—1 victory over Grimsby is shooting him right back into favour with the Welsh selectors.

'DROP ME'

SWANSEA boss Trevor March and wing half Mel Charles had a frank chat yesterday.

"I'm trying hard, but things just won't go right," Charles told Morris.

"What's worrying me as well is that people are saying that I'm playing badly just to get a move."

He asked for a spell in the reserves to restore his confidence.

But after the talk, Mel agreed to carry on in the first team—and killed any idea that he wants to leave Swansea.

"If I really wanted a transfer I should ask for one," he said.

TODAY'S GAMES

THIRD DIVISION
Rochdale v. Fremont (7.30).

FOURTH DIVISION (7.30).
Carlisle v. Barrow
Southport v. Port Vale (6.15).
Watford v. Chester

CENTRAL LEAGUE.—Burnley v
Preston (7.30).
SOUTHERN LEAGUE.—Kettering v
Zeta Camp.; Yeovil v. Trowbridge
Town

ABOVE: Johnny Carey's recruitment as manager made headline news.

LEFT: Manager Johnny Carey watches as Tommy Ring, accompanied by wife Sally, signs for Everton in January 1960.

Carey in action as a player for Manchester United in 1947.

Buchan's replacement, former Manchester United captain Johnny Carey, was something of a marquee appointment. After his playing career had come to an end in 1953, Carey had taken over as manager of Blackburn Rovers and guided them back into the First Division in 1958 after four near misses (including the 1953–54 season when Everton had won promotion at Blackburn's expense).

Since 1955 he had also combined his job at Ewood Park with managing the Republic of Ireland side, although he had little day-to-day involvement and the team was still chosen by a selection committee. Backed by ambitious chairman John Moores, who desired to return the club to the top of English football, Carey was able to attract big names to Goodison Park including the likes of Billy Bingham, Alex Young, Roy Vernon and Jimmy Gabriel.

But progress was still slow, with a fifth-place finish in the 1960–61 season about as good as it got for Everton and Johnny Carey, and it soon became apparent that a rift was growing between the manager, the Board and fans. Finally, in April 1961, with Carey and Moores in a taxi heading to a Football League meeting, the chairman informed the manager that his services were no longer required. The search was on once again for someone to take control at Goodison Park.

The Catterick Early Years
1961-1966

Everton's forwards keep fit in the snow in early 1962. Left to right: Bingham, Collins, Young, Vernon, Fell. Young, the so-called "Golden Vision", would contribute goals and guile to Harry Catterick's title-winning team the following year.

The 1960s was the decade in which Britain finally threw off the austerity of the postwar era and people from all walks of life began to express themselves with a sense of freedom and an (almost) anything-goes attitude. Football reflected the spirit of the times by embracing new ideas and new ways of playing, and Everton were a club at the forefront of this new way of thinking. The seeds of the club's revival were sown with the appointment of Harry Catterick as manager in the spring of 1961. The former Goodison man immediately set about restoring his club to pre-eminence. Tony Kay was signed for a club record £55,000 in 1962 as the rebuild continued, followed a year later with the £85,000 purchase of Fred Pickering. Pickering's goalscoring prowess helped steer Everton towards reward with the 1963 league title residing at Goodison. This was a new golden age for the club, with the youth team winning their cup competition in 1965 and further success for the first team to follow. But there were setbacks along the way in the rebirth of the Blues, notably Kay's conviction and ban for match fixing in 1964, stemming from his time as a player at Sheffield Wednesday. The team, however, was made of robust stuff and the FA Cup was won for the first time in 33 years in 1966: a great year for English football (with Goodison hosting World Cup matches) and confirmation that, at a time when the domestic game was wonderfully competitive with a large number of sides having the potential for honours, Everton were firmly among the elite.

BELOW: Liverpool players look on dejected as Everton celebrate the Howard Kendall goal that won the February 1968 derby by the slimmest of margins.

69

According to some sections of the press, Everton were preferably looking for a former player to take over at Goodison Park, someone who would understand the history and heritage of the club. Those same sections of the media highlighted Joe Mercer as having the necessary credentials but, instead, the club opted to appoint Harry Catterick.

As a player Harry had been 27 years old when he finally got to make his first-team debut for the club in 1946; he had struggled to hold down a regular spot in the team for the next five years, subsequently moving to Crewe Alexandra in 1951.

Catterick had cut his managerial teeth as player-manager there for two years and then turned to full-time management with Rochdale in 1953.

His abilities on a shoestring budget did not go unnoticed, for, in 1958, he was appointed manager at Sheffield Wednesday as replacement for Eric Taylor. He achieved almost immediate success, taking the club to the Second Division title at the end of his first season in charge. The following term the Owls were semi-finalists in the FA Cup and then, in 1960–61, he guided them to the runners-up spot in the First Division, albeit some way behind Double-winners Tottenham.

By the time the league campaign finished, however, Harry Catterick had already been introduced to the media as the new manager of Everton. That was about the only time he spoke to the press, for while many of his contemporaries, in particular Bill Shankly, his rival across Stanley Park, went out of their way to provide quotes and information, Harry was introverted and secretive. He preferred giving out little or no details about his team or tactics; when he had to provide a team list, he did so with the players listed in alphabetical order so as not to give an indication of formation! He was also against televised football, preferring to keep Everton's playing style as much of a mystery as it could be.

RIGHT: Harry Catterick (standing) observes Everton players (left to right) Ray Wilson, Sandy Brown, Alex Scott and Jimmy Gabriel enjoying a cup of tea before flying out for a pre-season tour of Norway, August 1965.

–LEGENDS–

Harry Catterick

Former playing favourite Catterick was summoned to Goodison from Sheffield Wednesday in 1961 to replace Johnny Carey. Catterick had played for the club throughout the Forties and in the early Fifties, scoring 24 league and cup goals in 71 matches.

His predecessor left him Roy Vernon, Alex Young and Jimmy Gabriel, so Catterick built on that foundation and, with the shrewd addition of players such as John Morrissey, Fred Pickering and Ray Wilson, put together a side that finished fourth in 1962 and won the league in '63. This was followed by the FA Cup three years later, 3-2 against former club Sheffield Wednesday, and a less successful return to Wembley two years later.

Catterick's preference for cultured football brought Everton the nickname of the "School of Science". The 1970 title-winning team was built on the midfield backbone of Alan Ball, Harvey and Kendall, with Joe Royle up front banging in the chances they created.

Like Bill Shankly, Catterick was faced with rebuilding a successful Sixties side to face the new decade and, like his Liverpool counterpart, found this difficult if not impossible. Defeat to Panathinaikos in the European Cup in 1971 followed by a FA Cup semi-final reverse to Liverpool was the writing on the wall, and the team fell to 14th place only 12 months after heading the league. Catterick suffered a heart attack in January 1972, and in April 1973, with four years still left on his contract, continuing fears about his health forced a move "upstairs".

A private, secretive man in his dealings with the media, Catterick showed his ebullient side when celebrating the 1966 FA Cup victory.

> *Harry Catterick doesn't get the accolades he deserves.*
>
> Colin Harvey

FOOTBALL –STATS–

Harry Catterick

Name: Harry Catterick

Born: Darlington, 1919

Died: 1985

Position: Striker

Everton Playing Career: 1946–51

Everton Management Career: 1961–73 (Two league titles, one FA Cup)

Club Appearances: 71

Goals: 24

International Appearances: 0

Goals: 0

Striker and future Everton manager Billy Bingham wins a header from a cross by Mickey Lill, challenged by Burnley's Elder and keeper Blacklaw, in March 1962.

While Harry Catterick did not do much to cultivate an image outside the club, inside was a different story. Disciplined, thorough and methodical with a keen eye for a player and a propensity to spend the club's money as carefully as if it were his own, he quickly assembled a side that would play true to Everton's tradition of cultured and attacking football. More importantly, it was a side that delivered results.

Catterick's first full season in charge saw Everton compete at the right end of the table; had their away form been even half as good as their home performances, then Everton would have won the league. As it was, the 21 matches at Goodison Park produced 17 wins, two draws and just two defeats (a record only equalled by Ipswich). On their travels Everton picked up both points on only three occasions, drawing nine and losing the other nine matches. That left them in fourth place in the table, five points behind surprise champions Ipswich Town.

Their performances during 1961–62 were enough to earn Everton their first tilt at European football, entering the Inter-Cities Fairs Cup at the first-round stage. An early departure, however, meant Everton could concentrate on the job at hand, which was trying to win the league title.

Meanwhile new faces kept arriving at Goodison Park, with the likes of Gordon West, Dennis Stevens, Alex Scott, Tony Kay and Johnny Morrissey (the latter signed from Liverpool without the knowledge of Bill Shankly) joining home-grown talents such as Brian Labone, Brian Harris and Mick Meagan as a new Everton began to take shape.

Everton's gentle giant defender Brian Labone greets his schoolboy admirers after a round of golf at Bootle Golf Course, 1962. Everton made a number of shrewd signings during the decade, but it was a home-grown player like Labone that was to prove just as important to the success of the club.

The last of the great Corinthians.

Harry Catterick, on Brian Labone

Gordon West, absent through injury, celebrates in the stands as Everton win the league, May 1963.

That Title-Winning Feeling

Without the distraction of Europe, Everton soon found their way to the top of the table, where they became involved in a battle with Leicester City, Burnley and Tottenham in a four-way chase for the title. With Leicester and Burnley eventually falling by the wayside, it was down to a straight fight with Everton's London rivals, who were also still heavily involved in the European Cup Winners' Cup (which they were ultimately to win).

The key match came on 20th April when Spurs visited Goodison Park, where the second highest crowd of the season, 67,650, saw Alex Young score the only goal of the game to take Everton to the top of the table on goal average. They were not to be headed again, for a solid run in to the end of the season saw Everton finish six points ahead of the rest of the field and become champions for the sixth time.

That champagne moment. Liquid refreshment for the league winners.

Everton beat Fulham 4-1 on the last day of the season to rubberstamp the title. Roy Vernon scores one of his three goals.

ABOVE: Everton players take a well-earned lap of honour at the end of the match against Fulham.

LEFT: Players and management bask in the glory of collective triumph.

The players' reward for winning the league was a two-week holiday in Torremolinos, Spain, with their wives. Seen at Manchester Airport in May 1963 are Mr and Mrs Dennis Stevens, Gordon West and Brian Harris.

Everton boss Harry Catterick films his players with the Football League Championship trophy, 1963.

The title win would give Everton another crack at European football, this time in the European Cup during the 1963–64 season. The significance of European football was rapidly becoming apparent. Once again, however, Everton's campaign fell at the first hurdle, beaten 1-0 on aggregate by eventual winners Inter Milan.

Everton versus Inter Milan in the European Cup preliminary round, September 1963. Dennis Stevens, the only ever-present Evertonian in all competitions that season, is challenged by Inter goalkeeper Sarti, who was injured in this incident. The first leg of the tie ended goalless but the Italians took the second to progress by the slenderest of margins.

DAILY MIRROR, Thursday, September 19, 1963   PAGE 31

THE END FOR EVERTON

Our European Cup hopes outwitted by slick Italians

By FRANK McGHEE

Everton 0, Internazionale (Milan) 0

EVERTON are out of the European Cup. Miracles don't happen in this class of competition.

And it will take a miracle to save them in the second leg of this qualifying round tie in the howling, screaming inferno of Milan's San Siro Stadium next Wednesday.

On last night's form they had nothing to stop Inter from brushing them aside, scoring the goals that will provide the final seal of the superiority the Italians showed at Goodison.

Certainly the muscle, the effort, the pace Everton poured into this first leg match never looked nearly enough.

Tactical Boob

The Italians were better, both tactically and individually. The finest players on the field all wore the black and blue of Internazionale.

And one of the greatest was the strutting Spanish inside left Louis Suarez, cool, controlled and rejoicing in the midfield space he was so unaccountably granted—just one of Everton's many tactical boobs.

The Italians set up a seven-man penalty area screen that Everton never really looked like penetrating. But our champions can't complain about it.

They knew in advance it would happen. They went out there knowing the tactics to beat it.

They had the speed of Alex Scott down the right wing, an asset that was never used because on the few occasions he made himself available he didn't get the service.

Everton's "tactics" seemed to consist mainly of hitting long balls that got lost in the forest of towering defenders planted inside Inter's penalty area.

The Italians managed more shots at goal than Everton, eleven against ten, won more corners, eight against six.

And an even more significant statistic is that the referee, a scrupulously fair Hungarian, Gyula Gere, awarded eighteen free-kicks against Everton, twelve against Inter.

He also booked Everton's left half Tony Kay in the fifty-seventh minute for allegedly treading on Suarez after flattening the great man in a fair tackle.

Offside

Twelve minutes from time Everton appeared to have earned at least a slim chance of survival when inside left Roy Vernon drove the ball home past goalkeeper Sarti.

But the roar of the 62,408 crowd was abruptly stilled when Mr. Gere ruled Vernon offside.

CASH NOTE: One consolation for Everton—the £31,450 receipts was a record "gate" for an English club.

Roy Vernon races in to slip the ball into the Internazionale net in the seventy-eighth minute—but it was no goal. Referee Gyual Gere ruled that Vernon was offside.

GREYHOUNDS

83

The two teams from either side of Stanley Park line up before the derby game, February 1964. Everton were looking to avenge a 2-1 defeat at Anfield, and goals by Jimmy Gabriel and Roy Vernon enabled them to bring their opponents' title charge to a temporary halt with a 3-1 victory.

With Liverpool now back in the top flight, the two derby games of the season were always eagerly awaited and hard-fought affairs, given added spice by the standing of both sides. Even if their neighbours were on their way to winning the title previously held by Everton, a derby victory at Goodison by Everton in the season's second meeting between the two on 18th February 1964 was a more than welcome sight for most of the crowd of 66,515.

RIGHT: Tony Kay holds back Liverpool's Ian St John after he appeared to have struck Gordon West. The keeper rolls on the ground holding his face, while Brian Labone points to West and Sandy Brown to St John.

Jimmy Gabriel gives Gerry Byrne a kick where it hurts as the derby tussle continues, even though the ball has gone out of play. While no quarter was given on the pitch, off-field relations were generally friendly.

85

Everton's season in 1963–64 came off the rails through no fault of their own. In 1964 the public around the country awoke to headlines revealing how three Sheffield Wednesday players had bet £50 each in December 1962 on their side to lose away at Ipswich Town. Ipswich had duly won 2-0, but disgruntled bookmakers who lost thousands in the betting sting were suspicious enough to launch an investigation.

It was eventually revealed that former Everton player Jimmy Gauld had been the ringleader and had involved a number of players, including former Swindon Town team-mate David Layne. In turn, Layne had involved fellow Wednesday players Tony Kay and Peter Swan. Both Kay and Swan were England internationals, with Kay having subsequently been transferred to Everton for £55,000 in December 1962.

All three players were punished by the courts before the football authorities could deal with the matter; Kaye was forbidden to even turn out for the Thorp Arch Open Prison team. Everton lost £55,000 on the player, while Kay lost his home (he was living in an Everton club house) and his career. Bizarrely, he had been named man of the match in the game he was supposed to have thrown.

RIGHT: Tony Kay was handed a four-month prison sentence after the bribes scandal. When he was released after 10 weeks it was to the news that the FA had banned him from football for life.

Kay, on his release from prison in April 1965. The touching family scene was not to last as Kay left his wife and children in the troubled aftermath of the scandal.

" *I loved football more than anything, and still do.*

Tony Kay, in 1997

"

Everton players leave for Sunderland in their new £10,000 coach ahead of their FA Cup fifth-round match in February 1964. Hopes of a run in the competition after the disappointment of European Cup defeat at the first hurdle were high. Having disposed of lowly Hull City after a replay in the third round and Leeds after another replay in the fourth, the Toffees returned from Roker Park with their tail between their legs after a 3-1 defeat.

EVERTON A.F.C. FIRST TEAM

Everton's third-place finish in 1963–64 was rewarded by a close-season tour of Australia. They took off from Speke (now John Lennon) Airport on 28th April to play a two-game series against the Australian national team.

Wives and girlfriends of the Everton team wave their last goodbye as the plane taking them to Australia departs …

The opening match of the series at Olympic Park in Melbourne saw Everton defeat the Australians by eight goals to two, with hat-tricks to Jimmy Gabriel and Roy Vernon and a Derek Temple double.

The second match of the tour saw the local national team suffer another heavy defeat. A double from Johnny Morrissey was augmented by Jimmy Gabriel, Colin Harvey and Alex Scott in a 5-1 victory at the Sydney Showground.

Everton's efforts also earned them entry into the Inter-Cities Fairs Cup for 1964–65 and, this time, they made it beyond the first round. Indeed they made it as far as the third, having seen off Vålerengen of Oslo and Kilmarnock before losing to Manchester United (so much for the international flavour of the competition!).

… before their husbands sample the delights of Sydney cricket ground during the club's tour of Australia, May 1964.

While the club were to slip only one place down the league table, they were 12 points adrift of Manchester United and Leeds United and seven points behind third-placed Chelsea at the end of 1964–65. Fourth place, however, did carry a return to Europe and the Inter-Cities Fairs Cup. This time they went out in the second round to Újpesti Dózsa, while 11th place in 1965–66 was Everton's worst league finish for six years.

The Everton squad for season 1964–65. Back row (left to right): Johnny Morrissey, Jimmy Harris, Sandy Brown, Brian Labone, Gordon West, Andy Rankin, Jimmy Gabriel, Fred Pickering, Colin Harvey and Jimmy Hill. Front row: Alex Parker, Alex Scott, Dennis Stevens, Derek Temple, Roy Vernon, Tony Kay, Alex Young and Ray Wilson.

Colin Harvey celebrates scoring a goal on his derby debut, the third in a 4-0 win at Anfield, on 19th September 1964.

Everton's Alex Young (right) is harried by Chelsea's Ron "Chopper" Harris (left) during a 3-1 defeat at Stamford Bridge in September 1965.

94

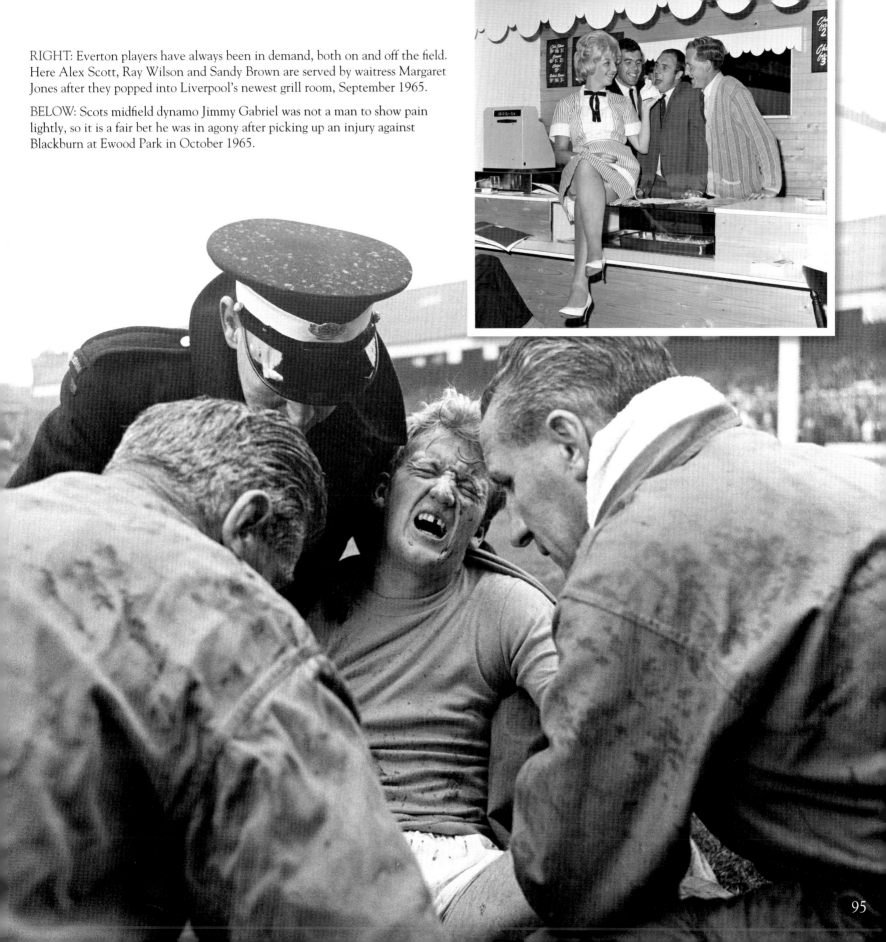

RIGHT: Everton players have always been in demand, both on and off the field. Here Alex Scott, Ray Wilson and Sandy Brown are served by waitress Margaret Jones after they popped into Liverpool's newest grill room, September 1965.

BELOW: Scots midfield dynamo Jimmy Gabriel was not a man to show pain lightly, so it is a fair bet he was in agony after picking up an injury against Blackburn at Ewood Park in October 1965.

The Everton squad pose at Goodison ahead of their FA Cup sixth-round replay against Manchester City, March 1966. The game ended goalless, so went to a second replay, which Everton won 2-0.

The real story of the 1965–66 season was the FA Cup. Mid-table for much of the league campaign, Everton came alive from January as Sunderland, Bedford Town, Coventry City, Manchester City (after two draws) and Manchester United were dispatched from the competition to give the Blues their first final at Wembley since 1933.

There they were to face manager Harry Catterick's former club Sheffield Wednesday, whose run to the final had been equally impressive. Catterick pulled something of a surprise in his team selection, selecting Mike Trebilcock, who had only recently returned from injury and had played just four reserve-team matches, ahead of England international striker Fred Pickering. Indeed, the selection was such a surprise that the official match programme hadn't bothered to include any mention of Trebilcock.

RIGHT: The *Mirror*'s headline reveals Harry Catterick's shock Cup final selection of Trebilcock over Pickering.

BELOW: Fred Pickering (dressed) drinks a toast to the players who have made sure of a Cup final place by beating Manchester United, little knowing he would not be taking part. The player with the cigar is Jimmy Gabriel, the one with champagne is Colin Harvey.

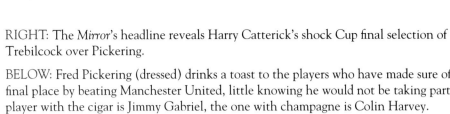

Everton had arrived at Wembley with an impeccable record: not one goal had been conceded in the earlier rounds, and this brought them in sight of a feat last achieved in 1902 by Sheffield United – winning the cup without conceding.

Watched by a crowd of 100,000, including, it is said, Paul McCartney and John Lennon of The Beatles, Everton managed to hold out for just four minutes before Jim McCalliog succeeded where others had failed. Twelve minutes into the second half David Ford doubled Wednesday's lead and the writing appeared to be on the wall.

Two minutes later, however, "mystery man" Mike Trebilcock pulled one back and, five minutes on, levelled the scores to set up a dramatic final half-hour.

The tension proved too much for some; Harry Catterick could hardly bear to watch the game, glancing instead at his watch as time ticked on.

The players at Lime Street station prepare to leave for Wembley to take on Sheffield Wednesday in 1966's showpiece domestic occasion.

HRH Princess Margaret meets the Everton players before the FA Cup final at Wembley Stadium, May 1966.

It is one of the most famous scenes from FA Cup final history, a clip forever replayed when the story of the grand old competition is recalled and remembered. Ecstatic Everton fan Eddie Cavanagh ran onto the field and was pursued by a posse of policemen, much to the delight of the spectators. When he was finally apprehended, with the aid of Brian Labone and Gordon West, Brian Harris picked up a dropped policeman's hat to try on. The break in play served to settle Everton more than it did Sheffield Wednesday.

Everton goalkeeper Gordon West punches clear from Fantham and McCalliog with Ray
Wilson standing guard on the goal line.

The victorious Everton team show off the cup on the Wembley pitch. England, of course, would be parading another trophy a matter of weeks afterwards, with future Evertonian Alan Ball at the heart of things.

Everton captain Brian Labone lifts the FA Cup after their victory on 14th May 1966.

With 15 minutes on the clock, Wednesday's stalwart defender Gerry Young failed to control a long downfield punt, which squirmed under his foot and into the path of Derek Temple. Evading a desperate lunging tackle, Temple headed towards the Wednesday goal and calmly slotted home the winner. Everton subsequently became only the second club to have won the cup in normal time after being two goals or more down.

–LEGENDS–

Brian Labone

The embodiment of the one-club loyalist, Brian Labone was the defensive rock upon which Everton's success of the 1960s was built. No other outfield player has played more times for the Toffees, and few others played with such consistency, class and good grace. In a 15-year career in blue, Labone was booked just twice.

A graduate of the youth "School of Science", Labone emerged as a commanding centre-half – not the formulaic muck-and-bullets type who would batter the ball and opponents with equal and undiscriminating ferocity, but a composed footballer who combined excellent technique and positioning with determination and an admirable level of physical commitment. "Labby" was an intelligent man who had turned down a place at university to focus on a professional football career and he brought a studious approach to the way he played, learning his craft and putting it into diligent practice.

By the time Labone was 20 he was a regular, and recognition for the national side soon followed, as he became the first Everton player to feature for England since the war. Though he was behind Bobby Moore and Jack Charlton in the pecking order by the time the World Cup swung round, Labone ruled himself out of contention for a squad place due to his wedding to Pat, a former Miss Liverpool. "I had fixed the date. What could I do?" he reasoned.

Made Everton skipper in 1964, Labone was to enjoy a long and happy engagement at Goodison Park (though he toyed with the idea of early retirement), leading the side to league and cup success before age and injuries called time on a singularly wonderful career.

Cutting a record in time-honoured footballer style in 1964, with Jimmy Gabriel, Jimmy Harris, Dennis Stevens, Alex Parker, Alex Scott and Sandy Brown.

Signing autographs for the fans at Euston station in 1969.

FOOTBALL -STATS-

Brian Labone

Name: Brian Labone

Born: Liverpool, 1940

Died: 2006

Position: Defender

Everton Playing Career: 1957–72

Club Appearances: 534

Goals: 2

International Appearances: 26

Goals: 0

Bringing the Cup Home

Scenes of jubilation outside St George's Hall in Liverpool city centre as crowds await the arrival of the victorious Everton team and the FA Cup.

Ever reticent to hog the acclaim, manager Harry Catterick shares the FA Cup trophy with a jubilant Brian Labone on the train journey back to Liverpool, May 1966.

Catterick with the Lord Mayor of Liverpool Alderman Cowley and the FA Cup trophy at Allerton.

New Looks, New Faces
1966-1972

FIFA had awarded the 1966 World Cup to England in August 1960, the victors fending off challenges from West Germany and Spain. By 1963, the FA had decided on their chosen venues for the tournament, with Goodison Park being selected to share Group 3 matches with Old Trafford. As it transpired, the ground hosted five games during the 1966 FIFA World Cup, including all three of Brazil's group fixtures.

The original schedule of the competition meant that if England won their group and then reached the semi-final, the match would be held at Goodison. But the organizing committee switched the venues, and West Germany played and beat the Soviet Union.

BELOW: Barricades come down and a reconfigured wall is erected at Goodison in preparation for the 1966 World Cup. Everton players in attendance to have a look at the changing shape of the famous old ground were Brian Labone, Gordon West, Mick Meagan, Dennis Stevens, Derek Temple and Alex Parker.

After the giddy successes of the first half of the 1960s, Everton had tailed off somewhat in the league and so Catterick set about restoring the side to challenge for the top honour. He began with the 1966 acquisition of Alan Ball; the midfield dynamo was to play a prominent part in the second phase of Catterick's reign. As well as improving the squad and the ground, Everton opened brand new training quarters in West Derby called Bellefield. Its facilities were state of the art at the time and were in use right up to 2011. A sixth-place finish in 1967 showed that progress was being made, beginning a steady rise up the table through the latter years of the decade. Though the FA Cup was lost in 1968, the reshaped team featuring Ball, Howard Kendall and Colin Harvey secured a seventh league title in 1970. Further success eluded the side, however, as the team began to break up. Ball was sold in 1971, and Catterick suffered a heart attack in 1972 before finally stepping down as boss a year later.

Fred Pickering, Alex Scott and Derek Temple try out the club's new Bellefield training headquarters in West Derby, March 1966.

While the FA Cup victory might have brought a change in European competition – in that a place in the European Cup Winners' Cup in season 1966–67 was the prize – it did not change Everton's performances on the Continent.

After elimination in the second round against Real Zaragoza, Everton slipped to sixth place in the league, while the defence of the FA Cup lasted as far as the sixth round. Nottingham Forest won 3-2, although the fifth-round clash against Liverpool, which Everton won 1-0, created a little bit of history. Such was the demand for tickets that a crowd of 64,318 crammed into Goodison Park while 40,169 were at Anfield to watch a closed-circuit television screening, making a total attendance of 104,487.

LEFT: Jimmy Gabriel, Alan Ball, Jimmy Husband and John Morrissey in dribbling practice at Bellefield ahead of their 1967 FA Cup match with Liverpool.

RIGHT: Liverpool chairman Syd Reakes (second right) and secretary Peter Robinson arrive at Goodison Park for the momentous meeting on whether to televise the upcoming FA Cup tie between Everton and Liverpool on closed-circuit television.

Derby Cup Fever

Police hold back large crowds of Everton fans desperate for tickets for their team's FA Cup fifth-round match against their local rivals. Fans queued for 35 hours before the turnstiles opened and the queue was a mile long down the Bullens Road and along Walton Lane.

Everton players and officials toast their FA Cup fifth-round victory in the dressing room.

–LEGENDS– Gordon West

Gordon West was Harry Catterick's first signing as manager, and turned out to be an inspired one. The Barnsley-born keeper had impressed with Blackpool, displacing the established Tony Waiters when still just 17, and went on to replace Albert Dunlop at Goodison and serve 12 seasons there. He was signed for £27,000, then a British record for a goalkeeper.

West played in four different Everton teams. In 1962–63 he won the Championship in his first season. Then came the 1966 FA Cup final, the loss in the final to West Brom in 1968 and the league title in 1970. Only two players got medals from all four of those achievements – West and Brian Labone.

Three ever-present campaigns belied the fact he was challenged for some time by Andy Rankin, while he attracted the attention of England manager Sir Alf Ramsey. Had West not declined the invitation to be part of the squad for Mexico World Cup in 1970 to be with his family then he, not Peter Bonetti, could have faced West Germany in the fateful quarter-final. As it was he earned three caps in the 1968–69 season as Gordon Banks ruled between the sticks.

Gordon West retired in 1973 after over 400 games for the Toffees, picking up his gloves again two years later for a brief and not very successful comeback across the Mersey with Tranmere Rovers. After giving up football, West worked in security and is now an after-dinner speaker.

West saves from Chris Lawler to safeguard Everton's 1-0 lead over Liverpool, February 1968.

FOOTBALL
–STATS–

Gordon West

Name: Gordon West

Born: Barnsley, 1943

Position: Goalkeeper

Everton Playing Career: 1962–73

Club Appearances: 402

Goals: 0

International Appearances: 3

Goals: 0

—LEGENDS— Joe Royle

A traditional English centre-forward in every sense, Joe Royle became the youngest ever Everton first-team player when he faced Blackpool in 1966 aged just 16; the record stood until James Vaughan beat it in 2005.

The four seasons between 1967 and 1971 saw Royle notch 95 goals in 190 appearances, notably scoring 23 goals while helping Everton to the 1970 Championship. Recognition from England followed, and he played for his country six times, scoring twice.

Joe Royle left for Manchester City in 1974 as Harry Catterick's team was broken up, and went on to achieve big things in 12 years as manager with Oldham Athletic, leading them into the top flight in 1991. But when he returned to his beloved Goodison as boss in late 1994, the club was ailing. He instilled a "Dogs of War" attitude in place of the previous "School of Science", sending out Duncan Ferguson to play in the role he himself once filled.

He took the club to FA Cup victory that season but could not sustain the success and left in 1997. Further managerial spells with Manchester City and Ipswich followed. Genial Joe is now a media pundit, having turned down further full-time managerial posts.

FOOTBALL —STATS—

Joe Royle

Name: Joseph Royle

Born: Liverpool, 1949

Position: Striker

Everton Playing Career: 1966–74

Club Appearances: 276

Goals: 119

International Appearances: 6

Goals: 2

Royle in typically committed action against Nottingham Forest in 1969.

Faces at the club continued to alter as Catterick rang the changes, with Alan Ball (front left) having joined in August 1966 from Blackpool for £110,000 after helping England win the World Cup that summer alongside Everton defender Ray Wilson. In March 1967 they were joined by Howard Kendall (stood up) from Preston for £85,000, with Ball and Kendall linking in midfield with the home-grown Colin Harvey (next to Ball). The partnership is still affectionately known at Goodison as the "Holy Trinity".

When Catterick was pursuing the signature of Howard Kendall, he gave an exclusive interview to a journalist stating that Everton had missed out on signing the player as he had opted to join Liverpool. By the time the newspaper concerned printed its exclusive on Kendall's transfer to Anfield, Kendall had in fact put pen to paper for Everton – Harry Catterick got one over Bill Shankly that day.

Harvey and Kendall, two thirds of the trinity, sign autographs for young fans.

Kendall scores the only goal of the derby game at Goodison, February 1968.

A B C D E F G H J K

How the *Daily Mirror* saw the Everton and West Bromwich squads before their Wembley face-off.

FA CUP FINAL 1968

Time is running out for Albion's skipper . .

GRAHAM WILLIAMS, West Bromwich Albion's skipper, steps out at Wembley today hoping for a change of luck—and the victory that will put the club back into European Soccer next season.

This is the fifth time the Welsh international left back has played at Wembley, and he has yet to finish on the winning side.

Three of his previous appearances have been for Wales, the other for Albion in the League Cup Final against Queen's Park Rangers 14 months ago.

By PETER INGALL

He has worn a red shirt each time, but today he plays in white—Albion's lucky Cup strip.

Williams, 29, told me: "We shall win this time. It MUST be my turn to be lucky.

"I forecast back in January that we would win the Cup this season, and I'm confident that we are playing well enough to look after Everton. They are favourites, but favourites often slip up at Wembley."

HIS FAN!

As a kid Williams was an Everton supporter. "Back home in Rhyl everyone is Everton daft. I couldn't face the folks if we lost," he said.

One supporter with a special interest in the skipper is his three-and-a-half-year-old daughter Katherine, who is to sit in the stand with her grandmother. Graham's wife, Heather, will be with the Albion party.

Williams said: "Some people may think Katherine is young to see a match of this type, but this could be my last trip to Wembley as an Albion player and we want her to share in the occasion."

One player breaking his Wembley duck is centre half John Talbut, who has been there four times without playing.

He was reserve for England schoolboys against West Germany, on the fringe of the Burnley team that played Spurs in the 1962 Final, reserve for England against Wales, and Cup-tied when Albion lost to Q P R.

Talbut cracked: "It may be a coincidence that this is my fifth trip and I wear the No. 5 shirt. It could also be an unlucky omen for Everton."

Albion look to 34-goal centre forward Jeff Astle—he has scored in every round—to ease dressing-room tension.

"His jokes keep us all laughing, and we are hoping he'll be in cracking form on and off the field," said Williams.

What a great day it will be if Albion win the Cup in Alan Ashman's first season as their manager!

The former chicken farmer has guided his team without seeking publicity or headlines.

TRIBUTE

One of the best tributes paid to him was by Carlisle chairman Edmund Sheffield when he left to join West Brom. Sheffield said: "We had to face the fact that his ability is greater than Carlisle's potential."

Ashman, a free-scoring centre forward with Nottingham Forest before a knee injury cut short his career, has picked Albion off the floor after a disastrous start to the season, and has instilled in them a great will to win that has shown tremendously in their Cup run.

I feel that his driving power for success will pay off today, with Albion taking the Cup back to the Hawthorns for the first time in fourteen years.

EVERTON

Amber shirts; Blue shorts.

KICK-OFF 3 p m. Extra time if necessary. (Replay at Hillsborough, Thursday, 7.30)

1 GORDON WEST.—6ft. 1in.; 13st. 12lb. Joined Blackpool in March, 1960. Moved to Goodison for a then British record fee for a goalkeeper, £27,500 on March 26, 1962. Born Darfield. Played in Everton's 1965-6 Cup winning side v Sheffield Wednesday.

2 TOM WRIGHT. — 5ft. 8in.; 11st. 10lb. Former Liverpool schools' representative. Signed professional March 6, 1963. League debut at Blackpool, October 17, 1964. Born Liverpool, England Under-23 international. Played in 1966 Wembley side.

3 RAY WILSON.—5ft. 7in.; 10st. 7lb. Born Shirebrook, made his debut for Huddersfield in 1955-6. Made over 250 appearances before joining Everton on June 30, 1964. A member of the England World Cup-winning side. Played in 1966 Wembley team.

4 HOWARD KENDALL.—5ft. 8in.; 11st. Cost record fee for a half back of £80,000 when Harry Catterick signed him from Preston on March 18, 1967. Youngest player ever in a Wembley Cup Final, when he played for Preston v West Ham in 1964 at 17.

5 BRIAN LABONE.—6ft. 1in.; 12st. 11lb. Captain. Joined club at 17. Debut at Birmingham February 2, 1959. Over 350 appearances. Captain of the 1966 side and the League-winning side in 1963. Liverpool born.

6 COLIN HARVEY.—5ft. 7in., 11st. Liverpool born. Signed professional October 24, 1962. Debut in Italy v Inter-Milan September 23, 1963. League debut v Manchester United September 14, 1964. Member of the 1966 Wembley side.

7 JIMMY HUSBAND.—5ft. 9in.; 11st. England schoolboy international. Played for Newcastle boys. Moved to Goodison straight from school. Signed professional October 19, 1964. Debut April 19, 1965, at Fulham.

8 ALAN BALL.—5ft. 7in.; 10st. Red-haired dynamo, key member of England's World Cup side. Missed semi-final through suspension. Born Farnworth, near Bolton. Cost £110,000 from Blackpool on August 15, 1966. Top scorer last season.

9 JOE ROYLE. — 6ft.; 12st Nineteen-year-old Liverpool-born centre forward. Product of the club's junior sides. Played for England Youth team. Strong bustling leader with a strong shot in both feet.

10 JOHN HURST.—5ft. 10in.; 12st. 4lb. Blackpool-born defender who plays a dual centre half role with Labone. England Under-23 international. League debut at centre forward v Sheffield Wednesday, August 31, 1965.

11 JOHN MORRISSEY.—5ft. 7in.; 11st. 10lb. Signed for Liverpool when he left school. Liverpool debut in 1957. Moved to Everton on August 23, 1962, for £15,000 after thirty-five appearances. Everton debut August 25, 1962, v Sheffield Wednesday.

12 ROGER KENYON.—6ft.; 12st. Like Hurst, joined Everton from Blackpool schoolboys. Stood in for him in the semi-final and played brilliantly. Made his debut only four months ago and at 19 looks the ideal man to take over from Labone when he retires.

WEST BROMWICH ALBION

White shirts; White shorts.

Sketches by SALLON

1 JOHN OSBORNE.—6ft. 2½in., 12st. 4lb. England Schoolboys international at half back, joined Chesterfield on leaving school. Made League debut during the 1960-1 season in goal. Cost Albion £15,000 fee on January 6, 1967. Born Barlborough, Derbyshire.

2 DOUG FRASER.—5ft. 8in.; 11st. 6lb. Scottish international, joined club from Aberdeen on September 17, 1963, for £25,000. Made debut the next day against Birmingham. Born Eaglesham, near Glasgow. Member of Scottish touring party last summer.

3 GRAHAM WILLIAMS.—5ft 7in.; 12st. 6lb. Captain. Twenty-eight international caps for Wales. Signed professional in April, 19 5, as a winger, made his debut v Blackpool November, 1955 Gained a regular place at left back in 1959.

4 TONY BROWN.—5ft. 10in.; 11st. 7lb. Oldham-born, club's top scorer in 1965-6. Converted into an attacking wing half after several seasons in the front line. League debut at Ipswich September 28, 1963. Member of the England Youth side in 1963.

5 JOHN TALBUT.—6ft. 1½in.; 13st. Joined Burnley from school, and after nine seasons and over 150 games he moved to Albion for £25,000 on December 22, 1966. Played alongside Osborne in England Schoolboys side. In 1964 he gained seven Under-23 caps.

6 JOHN KAYE—5ft. 10in.; 12st. 1lb. Moved into defence when Ed Colquhoun was injured recently. Cost club a record fee of £45,000 from Scunthorpe on May 30, 1963. Born in Goole. Midland Player of the Year in 1965.

7 GRAHAM LOVETT, 5ft. 10in.; 10st. 4lb. Snatched from Birmingham City's nursery school and became full-time professional on November 11, 1964. Broke his neck seventeen months ago in car crash. Returned to side in replay against Colchester.

8 IAN COLLARD.—5ft. 7in.; 11st. Born South Hetton. Joined the club from school in Co. Durham. Debut v Burnley September 26, 1964, while still an apprentice. Versatile player, now used in a midfield role alongside Bobby Hope.

9 JEFF ASTLE.—5ft. 11in.; 11st 7lb. Native of Eastwood, Notts. Cost Albion £25,000 from Notts County on September 30, 1964. At Meadow Lane he played alongside Tony Hateley. He has scored eight Cup goals this season.

10 BOBBY HOPE.—5ft. 5in.; 11st. 4lb.. Albion's general. Joined the ground staff in 1959. Played for Scotland Schoolboys and now on verge of first full cap. Debut v Arsenal April 30, 1960, when he was only 16. Gained a regular place in 1964-5.

11 CLIVE CLARK — 5ft. 7in.; 10st. 7lb. Formerly on Leeds ground staff. Moved to Albion on January 4, 1961, from Q P R for £17,000. Debut v Preston January 14, 1961. Top scorer last season with 29 goals.

12 DENNIS CLARKE.—5ft 9in.; 11st. 7lb. Last-minute choice in last season's League Cup Final side that lost to Q P R. Born Stockton-on-Tees. Made his debut last Christmas v Spurs. Turned professional in 1965.

The man who lives in Offside house

By HARRY MILLER

LEO CALLAGHAN, right, the referee at Wembley today, is forty-three, slim and slight. He comes from Merthyr Tydfil, is a children's welfare officer and lives in a house he has named "Offside."

And when he calls the two captains together today he will be achieving a life's ambition.

He said: "There is nothing to compare with an FA Cup Final. It is the dream of every referee to get the honour. Now I have . . . and it feels great.

"I've been thinking about the Final, and looking forward to it, since first hearing over my car radio two weeks ago that I had been given the game."

Callaghan will be one of the smallest men on the pitch today. But his stature, after fourteen seasons on the Football League's list of referees, is immense.

The soft-spoken Welshman is no stranger to Wembley. He was in charge of the England-Northern Ireland international there earlier this season.

Callaghan was also a World Cup referee there in 1966.

Last night, at his London hotel, he told me: "Earlier this week, I had charge of the Welsh Association of Boys' Clubs Under-14 final. There were fewer than a thousand people at the game.

"Tomorrow, it's the FA Cup Final, and 100,000 people at Wembley.

"Next Monday, I'm back at Merthyr for the local schoolboys' Under-11 final. I'll enjoy that, and put just as much into it, as the big one at Wembley.

"Refereeing is hard work . . but a wonderful life. I love it."

The linesmen today are John Homewood (Sunbury-on-Thames) and Walter Johnson (Kendal).

TV

BBC

11.15—Cup Final Grandstand. The Wembley scene.

11.30—Cricket: M C C v. Australians.

1.30—People at the match—introducing some of the personalities.

1.40—Fight of the week, Walter McGowan v. Alan Rudkin.

1.55—How the teams got there.

2.15—Meet the teams—film profiles of the players.

2.25—Wembley—community singing.

2.50—Presentation of the teams and the Cup Final. Cup presentation.

4.50—Meet the winners—interviews with the men of the match.

The Final is also in colour on B B C-2 from 2.30 to 5.0.

RADIO 3 (194m., 464m.).—Preview, 1.35 Commentary, 2.40 4.50

ITV

12.30—How the teams reache[d] Wembley—their strengths, weaknesse[s] and moments of drama.

12.40—All-star wrestling.

1.40—Meet the players, manager and some of the supporters of Wes[t] Brom and Everton.

1.50—Racing from Lingfield.

2.5—Match prospects with Ro[n] Greenwood and Billy Wright.

2.25—Racing from Lingfield.

2.35—The Wembley build-up.

2.50—The Cup Final—first half.

3.45—Half-time. Racing results.

3.55—The Cup Final—second half Cup presentation, followed by wrestling

LEFT: St John's Ambulance men and fans combine to remove a collapsed steel girder taken from the terraces during the match with Liverpool.

The "Holy Trinity" began to make their impact felt during the 1967–68 season, helping Everton reach Wembley again in the FA Cup after victories over Southport, Carlisle United, Tranmere Rovers, Leicester City and Leeds United, again helped by a miserly defence that had conceded only one goal on their run to Wembley. There would be only one goal in the final, too: Jeff Astle winning the trophy for West Bromwich Albion with an extra-time strike after Everton had dominated for large periods.

A Cup Half Full

LEFT: A pensive look at the Wembley pitch before the 1968 FA Cup final in 1968.

BELOW: Kendall glumly surveys a runners-up medal as Everton return home after losing the 1968 Cup final. Four years earlier, while with Preston North End, he had been the youngest ever player in a Cup final.

ABOVE: Local MP Bessie Braddock offers commiserations to Brian Labone and his wife Pat, at the Everton reception after the game.

LEFT: Everton players wave to loyal fans on the steps of St George's Hall in Liverpool city centre. Note the size of the crowd welcoming the team home after a defeat.

Gordon West turns butcher as he sizes up a joint of beef, watched slightly nervously by Tommy Wright, Brian Labone, Sandy Brown, Alan Ball and Howard Kendall.

Everton hold their annual photocall at their Bellefield training ground in West Derby, 24th July 1969. Trainer Wilf Dixon takes a few pictures of his own.

LEFT: It was not just the team that was taking on a different perspective. The Goodison Road Stand was partially demolished and rebuilt during the 1969–70 season, leading to this striking image of both old and new stands side by side. The match is with Crystal Palace, in August 1969.

ABOVE: Some Goodison aspects, however, remained timeless. In front of Archibald Leitch's famous Gwladys Stand, groundsmen try to clear the snow from the pitch two days before a match against Bristol Rovers in the FA Cup fifth round, February 1969.

Full-blooded commitment and effort from Alan Whittle in a match against Nottingham Forest.

Keith Newton, newly signed from Blackburn Rovers in December 1969, poses with new boss Harry Catterick. The recruitment of the England full-back helped strengthen a title-chasing team.

Tilt at the Title

Despite the disappointment of losing the Cup final, Everton in general and Ball, Kendall and Harvey in particular, began to hit top form in the following campaign, hauling Everton up from fifth to third place in the league.

The following season promised to be even better, for Joe Royle was now spearheading the attack and the side's consistency was an indication that the team pretty much picked itself. Indeed, West, Royle, John Hurst and Wright appeared in all 42 league matches, Johnny Morrissey missed only one and Alan Ball just five.

Johnny Morrissey is all smiles after scoring his second goal in Everton's 6-2 thrashing of Stoke in October 1969.

In the pale February sunshine, Alan Whittle's long-range effort beats Bob Wilson and gives Everton the equalizer in a 2-2 draw with Arsenal.

The following are reproductions of newspaper clippings from the Daily Mirror, Thursday, April 2, 1970.

PAGE 26 — DAILY MIRROR, Thursday, April 2, 1970

Everton celebrate their title win in champagne style.

EVERTON CHAMPIONS

By DAVE HORRIDGE: Everton 2, West Bromwich 0

EVERTON succeeded Leeds as League champions last night. As they surged to their seventh title they set a new club record of 63 points—two more than when they last won the title seven years ago.

QUOTES

Fans find new hero in goal ace Whittle

Now Tom builds with gold bricks

From PETER WILSON
Aarhus, Denmark, Wednesday

snowcem
-protection with great economy

The effect is dazzling!

£5-10-0

Underrated

On The Roof!

Confident

British girls crash out

MCC LET CARTWRIGHT PLAY FOR SOMERSET

By PETER LAKER

PAGE 27 — DAILY MIRROR, Thursday, April 2, 1970

..AS LEEDS CRACK

By KEN JONES: Leeds 0, Celtic 1

LEEDS lost their way in the European Cup last night playing like a team that have finally over-reached themselves in a season of immense effort and ambition.

Quick-fire Celtic make life tough for Revie's men

George Connelly (left) turns in triumph as he beats Gary Sprake to put Celtic ahead.

WE'LL STILL WIN, INSISTS MERCER

From BOB RUSSELL: Gelsenkirchen, Wednesday
Schalke 1, Manchester City 0

Birchenall is chasing a Cup 'miracle'

By NIGEL CLARKE

Now it's tough for Watford

Complaint

Staggered

LATE GOAL SENDS COLCHESTER'S HOPES CRASHING

Chester 1, Colchester 0

Last night's results

EUROPEAN CUP

CUP WINNERS' CUP

FAIRS CUP

FIRST DIVISION

SECOND DIVISION

THIRD DIVISION

FOURTH DIVISION

THE CUP FINAL BOOK

PLAYBOY!

SPASTIC LEAGUE CLUB

SPORTS SUMMARY

GREYHOUNDS

SPEEDWAY

AMUSEMENTS & ENTERTAINMENTS

CINEMAS

"Talk about a fixture pile-up — they're waiting to take us on when you're finished!"

With a settled side, Everton started the 1969–70 season in fine form and maintained this right through to April, chased for most of the time by Leeds United. To be fair to Leeds, they were caught at the end of the campaign by a fixture pile-up, the consequence of extended runs in the FA Cup (they were beaten in the final) and European Cup (beaten semi-finalists). But in reality Everton were in majestic form throughout and fully deserved the title, finishing just one point behind the record haul for the division of 66 points.

The battle between Catterick's Everton and Revie's Leeds was great copy for football writers.

Winger Johnny Morrissey celebrates winning the League Championship title in the Goodison Park dressing room after beating West Bromwich Albion 2-0.

Champagne Blues: Players, manager and chairman celebrate winning the league title for the seventh time.

–LEGENDS–

Alan Ball

Lancashire-born "Bally" was the son of a professional footballer/manager, also named Alan, but eclipsed his dad in every respect by becoming a World Cup winner with England in 1966. The fiery 21-year-old midfielder with a temper to match his red hair then moved on to Everton, where his midfield partnership with Colin Harvey and Howard Kendall was the basis on which the 1970's title-winning side was built. An opening sequence of just one defeat in 18 fixtures provided the platform for Championship success and his £110,000 fee was adjudged a bargain.

A British record fee of £220,000, exactly double Everton's outlay, tempted him to Highbury at the end of 1971 and while he became the captain of Don Revie's England team he failed to win further domestic honours. After joining Southampton in 1976 and helping them to the top flight, Ball spent time in the North American Soccer League before returning to start a managerial career with the likes of Portsmouth (twice) and Manchester City that proved notably less successful than his playing record. He died in 2007 after a heart attack at the age of only 61.

Ball's 251 Everton appearances yielded a highly impressive 79 goals – he regularly hit double figures from midfield – while 39 of his 72 England caps were collected as a Blue. The fact he went on to play 400 games elsewhere underlines the fact that his sale was one of Everton's biggest misjudgements. His red hair, white boots and shrill voice made him an unmissable presence on the pitch – and how Everton missed him in the unsuccessful Seventies.

" Once Everton has touched you nothing will be the same.

Alan Ball "

Alan Ball treads the Goodison Park turf for the last time on the eve of his transfer to Arsenal, December 1971.

FOOTBALL –STATS–

Alan Ball

Name: Alan Ball

Born: Farnworth, 1945

Died: 2007

Position: Midfield

Everton Playing Career: 1966–71

Club Appearances: 251

Goals: 79

International Appearances: 72

Goals: 8

Ball with two of his soon-to-be erstwhile team-mates, John Hurst (left) and Roger Kenyon, after his last training stint with Everton.

ABOVE: Alan Ball serves as photographer at the wedding of his team-mate Howard Kendall (right) and 22-year-old Cynthia Halliwell at a church in Fulwood, near Preston, May 1970. Ball and club were soon to part.

RIGHT: A swansong from Ball as he celebrates his goal in the 1971 FA Cup semi-final at Old Trafford with team-mates Tommy Wright, Alan Whittle and Howard Kendall. Note Ball's famous white boots.

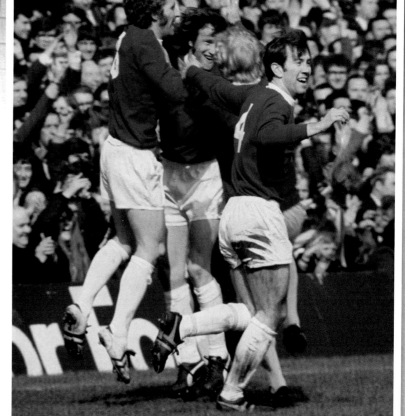

Surprisingly, the title win of 1970 proved to be the peak for what many Evertonians claim to be the best side to have represented the club during its history. The Toffees plunged down the league in 1970–71, finishing below halfway, and were never in with a shout of retaining the title.

The cups offered some respite, as the Blues reached the quarter-finals of the European Cup before going out to the surprise package of Panathinaikos on away goals, just a few days after Everton lost an FA Cup semi-final against Liverpool. Months later the "Holy Trinity" was no more as Alan Ball joined champions Arsenal for £220,000, a sale that effectively saw the end of Everton as a dominant force for several years.

On key in the studio for a recording of *Forever Everton* in 1972, but not quite as on key on the pitch.

Their 14th-place finish of 1970–71 was followed by consecutive 17th-place conclusions to 1972 and 1973. The strain of it all began to tell on Harry Catterick, who suffered a heart attack in January 1972 with the stress of trying to return the club to former glories. Eventually, in April 1973 he was persuaded to step down, becoming a non-executive director of the club and holding the position until he accepted the invitation to become Preston North End manager in August 1975. Despite this brief sojourn at Deepdale, Harry's heart and soul remained at Goodison Park; he was to die from another heart attack shortly after watching his beloved Everton draw 2-2 with Ipswich in an FA Cup quarter-final in 1985.

LEFT: Another stroke of bad luck for Catterick as Mike Bernard is carried off the pitch after being injured by Manchester United's John Fitzpatrick in a brutal clash at Goodison Park. Everton won the game 2-0 in August 1972, but by the end of that season the Catterick reign was over.

RIGHT: Everton could still produce some devastating performances, as poor Southampton and their keeper Eric Martin found to their cost in November 1971.

For the cause: John Morrissey showed just what the Merseyside derby meant to the players with this display of bloodied commitment in March 1971.

Change and Challenges
1973-1980

The hair may have got longer but the rhythms of football remained the same. In the post-Catterick era, a new-look team and management lined up in July 1974 for the usual pre-season photocall. Back row, left to right: John Smith, Dave Irving, Peter Scott, Dai Davies, Gordon West, David Lawson, Gary Jones, George Telfer and Billy Kenny. Middle row: First-team trainer and coach Stewart Imlach, John Hurst, Jim Pearson, Joe Royle, Mike Lyons, Bob Latchford, John Connolly and Ray Henderson. Front row: Dave Clements, Mike Buckley, John McLaughlan, Terry Darracott, manager Billy Bingham, Roger Kenyon, Mike Bernard, Steve Seargeant and Colin Harvey.

The rebuilding of Everton during the rest of the 1970s proved to be an elusive task as other sides began to dominate. What made Everton's labour all the harder was that it was Liverpool who were to emerge as the pre-eminent force. Former player Billy Bingham returned to Goodison to take over the reins of management in August 1973. Howard Kendall had become captain but was sold in 1974 and with Colin Harvey following suit out of the Goodison exit door, the "Holy Trinity" was no more. While Harvey's final days at Everton had been punctuated by injury, in particular a hip injury that was to eventually end his career, Kendall surely had much left to offer, as 276 league appearances for Birmingham, Stoke City and Blackburn Rovers after his departure from Goodison indicated. There were, of course, new arrivals. Everton showed they still had considerable spending power with a British record purchase of Bob Latchford, joining other new players such as Martin Dobson and Dave Clements. By the 1974–75 season the signs were promising and it seemed like an eighth league title was surely destined for Goodison (indeed several bookmakers had stopped taking bets) until a collapse in form with only seven points in their last eight matches ruined the Toffees' chances. 1977 proved to be a pivotal year of near misses and more changes. The team reached its first League Cup final but was defeated by Aston Villa, while Everton were controversially denied a place in the FA Cup final after defeat to Liverpool. Bingham ended his tenure as boss that year and was replaced by Gordon Lee. Big money signings such as Asa Hartford and John Gidman in 1979 illustrated continuing ambition, but the side could not deliver and a lowly finish in the 1979–80 season showed how far Everton had declined. Fourth from bottom, one place above the relegation places and just four points away from the drop was a sure indication that further change was in the offing.

ABOVE: A disgusted Roger Kenyon queries a linesman after Derby County's second goal, in September 1973. Manager Billy Bingham looks on as Everton lose 2-1.

LEFT: Flying winger Ronnie Goodlass hammers in a shot past Colin Todd in a First Division match in 1977 at the Baseball Ground against Derby County. Everton won 3-2.

After the near miss of 1974–75, the following season was little short of a major disaster. Both the UEFA Cup and FA Cup were exited at the first hurdle and an extended run in the League Cup was brought to a shuddering halt at Notts County. In the league Everton slipped down to 11th place, well short of expectations.

Worse, if at all possible, was the fact that, while Everton were seemingly on a downward spiral, their closest rivals were going in the opposite direction, winning both the league title and the UEFA Cup. Indeed it was the endless comparisons with what was happening at Anfield that added to the pressure on Billy Bingham and, it has to be said, on future managers.

Both clubs had replaced their managers at the same time, Billy Bingham taking over from Harry Catterick and Bob Paisley stepping into Bill Shankly's place. For Liverpool the transition had been seamless, but at Goodison Billy Bingham had struggled to build on the solid foundations laid by Harry Catterick, with just one sustained title challenge all he had to show for his efforts.

Everton came away from Highbury with a 2-2 draw in March 1975. Here Arsenal's John Radford shoves keeper Dai Davies in the back, to little effect.

Winger John Connelly makes his comeback from injury following a broken leg. Here he is in action against the Manchester City A team at Bellefield in December 1975.

As the 1976–77 season got underway, Everton found themselves in the wrong half of the table and could only watch helplessly as their neighbours mounted a challenge on three fronts, winning both the league title and European Cup and finishing runners-up in the FA Cup. By the time the trophies came to be handed out, Everton had already parted company with Billy Bingham, bringing his spell in charge to an abrupt end on 10th January 1977.

Given the success he had in his later managerial career, it may well have been that Bingham's style of management was perhaps better suited to the international game; there was never any criticism of his day-to-day handling of the team or other club matters, but he proved better able to motivate on the international stage than domestically.

Gordon Lee came to Goodison from St James' Park. He was said to be an archetypal modern manager, appearing at every training session and dealing with players on an individual basis, ensuring that each knew what he was supposed to be doing during the course of a game.

> *I don't drink, don't smoke and I'm getting fed up with gardening. I've no interests at all apart from football and family.*
>
> Gordon Lee after his spell at Everton

–LEGENDS–

Martin Dobson

The signing of England midfielder Martin Dobson from Burnley in the summer of 1974 for a near-record £300,000 was a statement of intent by Everton. (They had already paid Birmingham City £350,000 for the services of Bob Latchford a few months earlier, though Dobson's was the highest cash-only fee.)

However, Dobson's five-year stay coincided with a poor spell for the club and he would only add one more England cap to his total of four. He only missed 20 games but he could not help the team bag a trophy. The closest he came to a winner's medal was in his first season when the team finished fourth, just three points behind Derby County, and then two years after that in 1977 when the FA Cup semi-final and League Cup final were both reached but lost.

Dobson played 190 league games in blue, scoring 29 goals, and was the playmaker of the side alongside the aggressive Andy King. His lung-busting box-to-box running capacity, physical strength and quality marked "Sir Dobbo" out as a thoroughbred. Dobson returned to Burnley for £100,000 before taking over as Bury's player-manager in 1984. Brief spells as manager of Northwich Victoria and Bristol Rovers preceded another return to Turf Moor to become Burnley's head of youth development. In 2007 he published a football-based novel, titled *Ultimate Goals*.

Martin Dobson celebrates a goal. His career did not start off as anticipated at Goodison, but he was a loyal servant over his five years in blue.

FOOTBALL –STATS–

Martin Dobson

Name: Martin Dobson

Born: Blackburn, 1948

Position: Midfield

Everton Playing Career: 1974-79

Club Appearances: 230

Goals: 40

International Appearances: 5

Goals: 0

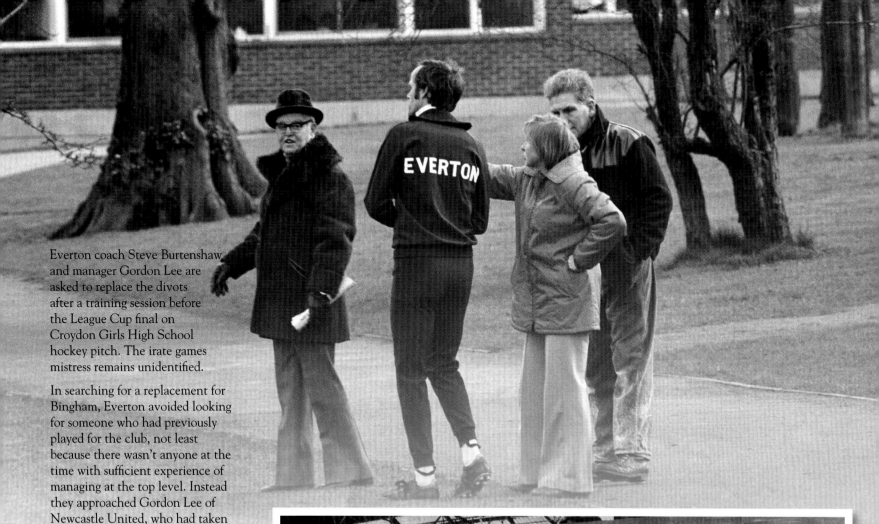

Everton coach Steve Burtenshaw and manager Gordon Lee are asked to replace the divots after a training session before the League Cup final on Croydon Girls High School hockey pitch. The irate games mistress remains unidentified.

In searching for a replacement for Bingham, Everton avoided looking for someone who had previously played for the club, not least because there wasn't anyone at the time with sufficient experience of managing at the top level. Instead they approached Gordon Lee of Newcastle United, who had taken the Geordies to the final of the League Cup in 1976 after having previously been in charge at Blackburn Rovers.

Lee arrived at Goodison with the club already through to the semi-finals of the League Cup, a competition that Everton had (and continue to have) a pitiful record in. Indeed, having competed in the very first competition in 1960–61, Everton had then refrained from entering until it was made compulsory! Bolton Wanderers were successfully overcome 2-1 on aggregate in the semi-final (although, in typical Everton fashion, they had contrived to draw the first leg at home and then won away) to earn Everton a surprise trip to Wembley to face Aston Villa.

The wives, girlfriends and children of the Everton side ready to board the train at Lime Street, en route to Wembley and the 1977 League Cup final.

154

Eight of the Everton side to play in the League Cup final against Aston Villa pictured in the goalmouth at Wembley. Telfer, Kenyon, Jones, McNaught, Lawson, Darracott, an Everton fan, and Barnard leaning against the goal post.

decide the 1977 League Cup.

How much the Wembley trip owed to Billy Bingham's cavalier approach as opposed to Gordon Lee's more methodical way of doing things is open to debate, but the end result was a dreary stalemate at Wembley. It wasn't much better in the replay at Hillsborough, which ended 1-1 and necessitated a third meeting at Old Trafford. As the Football League had already announced that the result would be decided on the night, by penalties if necessary, both teams played with a little more spirit than had been evident in their two earlier meetings.

RIGHT: Ken McNaught looks on as Villa attack the Everton goal.

BELOW: Action in the Villa goalmouth during the League Cup final second replay at Old Trafford, 13th April 1977.

Mirror Sport

THE WINNING Racing Mirror PAGES 28, 29

Thursday, April 14, 1977   No. 22,768
Telephone: (STD code 01)—353 0246

8-1 NAP   6-4 NAP

BOUVERIE (Charles Fawcus) and TIM RICHARDS both napped Mrs. McArdy, 8-1 winner at Newmarket yesterday.

NEWSBOY (Bob Butchers) napped Boldboy 6-4.

EXCLUSIVE

Why I'll carry on clowning!

By DEREK RANDALL

Notts and England

LITTLE'S A CUP GIANT

FRANK McGHEE at Old Trafford

ASTON VILLA finally won — and deservedly won—the League Cup last night with a goal from Brian Little, their darting terrier of a striker, in the last minute of 5½ hours of football.

It has to be admitted that he got his goal only because one of Everton's exhausted defenders, full-back Terry Darracott, made a mess of what should have been a simple interception.

But that must not and does not disguise the fact that Villa are worth the place in Europe this victory brings them.

Those who half-felt, half-hoped that the third meeting of these two teams couldn't possibly produce less entertainment and excitement than the first two yawns were given brief encouragement at the start —but only brief.

The first minute alone threatened to shame the meagre quota of thrills provided in the earlier games.

First Everton centre-half Ken McNaught had to make a late tackle to prevent Brian Little getting through.

Fierce

Then, at the other end, Everton's tricky winger Ron Goodlass got past John Gidman for a fierce low shot that Villa keeper John Burridge was grateful to smother for a corner.

It seemed — again briefly—as though both teams had decided they were tired of the cat-and-mouse, safety - first tactics which had ruined the two previous occasions.

But, alas, it didn't last. Goodlass's shot seemed to be destined to become the only one on target in the whole first half—until a dramatic 38th minute.

LEAGUE CUP FINAL SECOND REPLAY

Aston Villa . . 3
Nicholl, Little (2)

Everton 2
Latchford, Lyons

H.-T.: 0—1.   54,749
After ex. time: 90 mins.: 2—2

It started with Villa centre-half Chris Nicholl booked for a foul on Everton centre - forward Bob Latchford.

From the Goodlass free-kick, McNaught at the far post nodded it back across the penalty area and Latchford, from close range, steered it in.

At last it came to life. It was almost 2—0 a minute later when striker Jim Pearson forced Burridge to a save at the foot of the post after weaving his way clear.

Then, at the other end, Everton keeper David Lawson had to make a couple of saves within two minutes.

First he went down successfully at Little's feet after a superb through ball from Dennis Mortimer. Then he saved a close-range

Not this time . . . Everton striker Bob Latchford is foiled as Aston Villa goalkeeper John Burridge gets up to save.

header from the same man after a Mortimer corner.

Villa, forced into a second-half situation which demanded all-out attack, did their honest best to oblige.

Signs that Everton's composure was fraying under the pressure were clear.

Wide

Once, when the defence was at fault in failing to pick up a long strong run by Mortimer which finished with a shot only just wide, two of their team almost came to blows.

Midfield man Bryan Hamilton had to dive in to separate Latchford and McNaught.

There were howls from the Villa fans for a penalty when Lyons brought down Little, who was looking more dangerous with every passing moment.

He had a good header saved from Graydon's corner in the 65th minute

and it seemed that Everton were dedicating themselves simply to survival.

Three goals in three minutes changed the whole game sensationally.

In the 80th minute from fully thirty yards out Nicholl equalised when he swung a left foot at the ball and saw it flash past Lawson to nestle in the corner of the net.

Within sixty seconds Villa went brilliantly in front after a marvellous individual run by Little, who beat two defenders before slotting his shot from a narrow angle past the advancing Lawson.

It seemed all over then, with Villa well-deserved winners.

But Everton in a counter attack forced a corner and from it Lyons, up in support, forced home a close-range header.

Now it really was desperation stuff from both teams.

Two teams who should have been sick and tired

— exhausted by their efforts and fed up with the sight of each other —still went at it full pelt in extra time.

Everton, who had done far less of the running, seemed the stronger.

But it was Villa who came closest to scoring when Little forced Lawson to a desperate grab at his near post.

By my watch there was only a minute left when Little scored the winner.

It came when a cross from Gordon Smith, who came on in extra time as a substitute for Gidman, crossed from the right.

SPEED ACE CRASHES

Birmingham speedway captain Richard Greer was last night taken to hospital with a suspected broken arm after colliding with the safety fence in the British League match with Reading last night. Reading won 41—37 thanks to maximums from Dave Jessup and John Davis.

TOMORROW

Spurs need four out of six

By HARRY MILLER

TOTTENHAM were last night facing the harsh reality that nothing less than four wins from their remaining six games will keep them alive in the First Division.

It would give one of the game's great clubs 35 points.

And in the most desperate dog-fight at the bottom for years, even that may not be enough.

Tottenham have home games against Sunderland, Aston Villa and Leicester to go. Villa, Stoke and Manchester City have to be faced away.

The realistic appraisal of chairman Sidney Wale after Tuesday's 1—0 defeat at Bristol City was: "There is still hope, but I must confess it is faint."

2 minutes of your time could bring £34,590* to your family.

A couple of minutes spent reading this advertisement and another minute spent filling in the coupon could be extremely important to your family.

The new Abbey Life Family Cover Plan provides protection for your family by ensuring not only a capital sum in the event of your death but also, should you die before your wife, a regular monthly income up to age of 55 which combined could add up to as much as £34,590*.

Furthermore, in the event of your wife's death you will receive £1000 a year tax free, to help deal with your family and domestic commitments.

The Plan also guarantees your family an income of £1000 a year if you're disabled and unable to work.

Your right to take out further insurance is guaranteed irrespective of your state of health.

And last, but by no means least, you can look forward to a capital sum on retiring at age 65. This could be as much as £10,000, assuming an average annual net growth, including re-invested income, of 7½%.

To find out more about the comprehensive protection you can receive for as little as £10.50p a month simply return the coupon below.

We'll pay the postage.

*Based on age 25 next birthday.

To: F. B. Page, Abbey Life Assurance Co. Ltd., Freepost, London EC4B 4BD. Telephone: 01-248 6740. Please let me have details. (Not applicable to Eire.)
Name
Address

DM/14/4/FCM

Abbey Life Family Cover Plan

© The Daily Mirror Newspapers Ltd., 1977

Printed and Published by THE DAILY MIRROR NEWSPAPERS Ltd. (01-353 0246) at, and for Mirror Group Newspapers Ltd., Holborn Circus, London, E.C1P 1DQ. Registered at the Post Office as a newspaper.

The *Mirror*'s back page spells out Everton's agony as they fall at the final hurdle.

Unfortunately for Everton, who were also engaged in a marathon FA Cup run that would end in a semi-final defeat – the team ran out of steam. Having taken the lead in the first half, Everton found themselves behind and staring defeat in the face when they got an equalizer. As extra-time headed towards its climax, Brian Little got on the end of a centre to net the winner for Villa. A final finish of ninth for Everton made a disappointing season even worse.

159

Players and fans alike joyously celebrate a goal during the epic 2-2 draw with Liverpool in the 1977 FA Cup semi-final. Referee Clive Thomas (left) controversially disallowed a late Bryan Hamilton strike, thus preventing what would have been a deserved win for the Toffees. Instead, Liverpool came through 3-0 in the replay.

We were better than them and it was as simple as that. Anyone who saw the game knows who was the better side.

Gordon Lee, on his semi-final frustrations

161

With Lee now imposing his own ideas on the team and Bob Latchford rediscovering his goalscoring form, Everton improved considerably during the 1977–78 season and were at or near the top end of the table for much of the campaign. Nottingham Forest ended up surprise champions that year while the following term, 1978–79, saw Liverpool top and Everton having to settle for fourth place, a good 17 points behind. Europe had offered little respite, with a second-round loss to Dukla Prague on away goals, and there were also early exits in the domestic cups.

LEFT: Free-scoring forward Bob Latchford celebrates after scoring his 30th goal of the season in the 6-0 win over Chelsea, April 1978.

RIGHT: Thumbs up from midfield hero Andy King, who scored the only goal in the derby match against Liverpool in October 1978.

King for a Day

Andy King shows off some of the skills that he used to wonderful effect in the Merseyside derby in October 1978. King's superb volley settled the match at Goodison and earned him enduring cult status. It was Everton's first derby victory in seven years and, at a time when Liverpool were all-conquering, gave Evertonians welcome bragging rights, particularly as it closed the gap between the two sides at the top of the table to just two points.

Near misses were to be as good as it got during Gordon Lee's time in charge. The 1980–81 season was Lee's last in charge at Everton, a final position of 15th hiding the fact that Everton were only three points away from relegation this time around.

If there were any plusses to be gained from Lee's four years in charge then it was the emergence of several key players, including Kevin Ratcliffe and Graeme Sharp, who would figure prominently in the immediate future. Despite the manager's popularity among the players, the club's slump was not something the Board could ignore or allow to continue and so, on 6th May 1981, chairman Philip Carter brought an end to Gordon Lee's managerial position at Goodison Park.

The Everton squad pictured before the 1979–80 season. An alarming slump saw the club finish just one place above the relegation spots, even if they were four points ahead of third-from-bottom Bristol City. An extended FA Cup run was halted by West Ham United in the semi-final after a replay, with West Ham on their way to becoming the last Second Division side to lift the trophy

Brian Kidd salutes after scoring Everton's fourth goal in the FA Cup tie against Aldershot, held at Goodison Park in January 1979. The veteran striker was one of Gordon Lee's buys, having played for both Manchester clubs and Arsenal, but failed to set Merseyside alight – at least against top-class opposition – and stayed only a season before moving on to Bolton.

–LEGENDS–

Bob Latchford

Striker Bob Latchford was unlucky enough to serve Everton in the 1970s, an era when he and they failed to win any significant honour. Yet he was a 6ft tall centre-forward in the Joe Royle tradition and won the admiration and affection of the supporters as well as a dozen England caps (scoring five goals).

He started his career in the Birmingham City team that featured brother Dave in goal (he had another professional goalkeeping brother, Peter). Howard Kendall was one of two players offered in part exchange when Latchford moved in February 1974 for a record £350,000. Deadly with his head and seemingly fearless, he fought for most of his 138 goals and brought Toffees' fans comfort in a dreary decade. The closest he came to a winner's medal at Everton was a finalist in the three-game League Cup final in 1977, equalizing in the replay and scoring the first goal in the second replay.

Latchford topped Everton's club goalscoring charts for six successive seasons but it was in 1977–78, when he won a national newspaper prize as the first man to score 30 league goals in a season, that he shot to national acclaim. He scored twice against Chelsea in the final game to take the prize, fittingly within days of the 50th anniversary of Dixie Dean's 60-goal season. He remained second to Dean in the club's all-time scoring chart until overtaken by Graeme Sharp in 1989.

Latchford signed for Swansea in 1981 and scored a hat-trick on his debut as they graced the top flight of English football for the first time. He later played in Holland, ending his playing days back in Wales with non-league Merthyr Tydfil in 1986–87. Now living in Germany, Bob makes regular return trips to England to speak on the after-dinner circuit.

ABOVE: Everton were splashing the cash in the mid-Seventies, and Birmingham's Bob Latchford was their record buy.

RIGHT: The thoroughbred footballer Bob Latchford poses beside a thoroughbred Rolls-Royce.

Latchford mobbed by jubilant fans after scoring his 30th goal of the 1977–78 season in a 6-0 win over Chelsea.

FOOTBALL
–STATS–
Bob Latchford

Name: Robert Latchford

Born: Birmingham, 1951

Position: Striker

Everton Playing Career: 1974–81

Club Appearances: 289

Goals: 138

International Appearances: 12

Goals: 5

Kendall to Royle
1981-1995

A generation on from when he was a player, Howard Kendall celebrates the second of his two titles as Everton boss.

The man charged with the task of restoring Everton to former glories had served his managerial apprenticeship with great distinction at Blackburn Rovers, earning promotion from the Third Division in 1979–80 and coming within a whisker of promotion to the First Division (Rovers missed out on goal difference). Such success made Kendall a coveted boss, and he was installed at Goodison as player-manager in 1981. Kendall's remodelling of the side began in earnest with the signing of Adrian Heath in 1982, joined by Kevin Sheedy and Peter Reid, with Trevor Steven and Andy Gray becoming Toffeemen a year later in 1983. Despite the setback of losing the League Cup final to the arch enemy in 1984, confirmation of Everton's revival came with victory in the FA Cup the same year. In 1985 the most glittering domestic prize of all, the league title, was once again secured, the trophy taking pride of place in the cabinet along with the club's first European trophy, the Cup Winners' Cup, but Everton just missed out on a famous treble with defeat in the FA Cup final. Everton were now the best side in the country and potentially the best side in Europe, but the ban on English clubs resulting from the Heysel Stadium disaster meant the team were denied the opportunity to prove just how good they were up against the Continent's finest. 1986 proved to be something of a nearly season, as Everton just missed out on winning the League and Cup Double, and record signing Gary Lineker left after just one prolific season at Goodison. Kendall's team recovered to win the title once again in 1987 but the man who had engineered Everton's revival stunned the football world with his resignation the same year. His assistant and former "Holy Trinity" colleague Colin Harvey took over and while he and the team just missed out on another FA Cup in 1989 the cycle of magnificent success was drawing to a close. Kendall provided another twist in the tale by returning to Goodison in 1990 and restoring the double act with Harvey, but the pair could not rekindle former glories. As the Blues slumped, Mike Walker took over but nearly suffered the ignominy of being the man who took Everton down to the second tier, but for a last-gasp win in 1994. Instead it fell to another former Everton favourite to try and rediscover the winning formula, with Joe Royle proving a success by steering Everton to FA Cup victory in 1995, to date Everton's last major trophy.

The successful 1985 Everton team, and their manager Howard Kendall, pose for a group photograph on the pitch at Goodison Park with their trophies, including the Charity Shield, the League Championship trophy and the European Cup Winners' Cup trophy in August 1985. Back row, left to right (players only): Pat van den Hauwe, Derek Mountfield, Bobby Mimms, Neville Southall, Paul Wilkinson and Paul Bracewell. Middle row: Gary Stevens, Graeme Sharp, Alan Harper, Gary Lineker, Neil Pointon and Ian Atkins. Front row: Peter Reid, John Bailey, Kevin Sheedy, Kevin Ratcliffe, Trevor Steven and Adrian Heath.

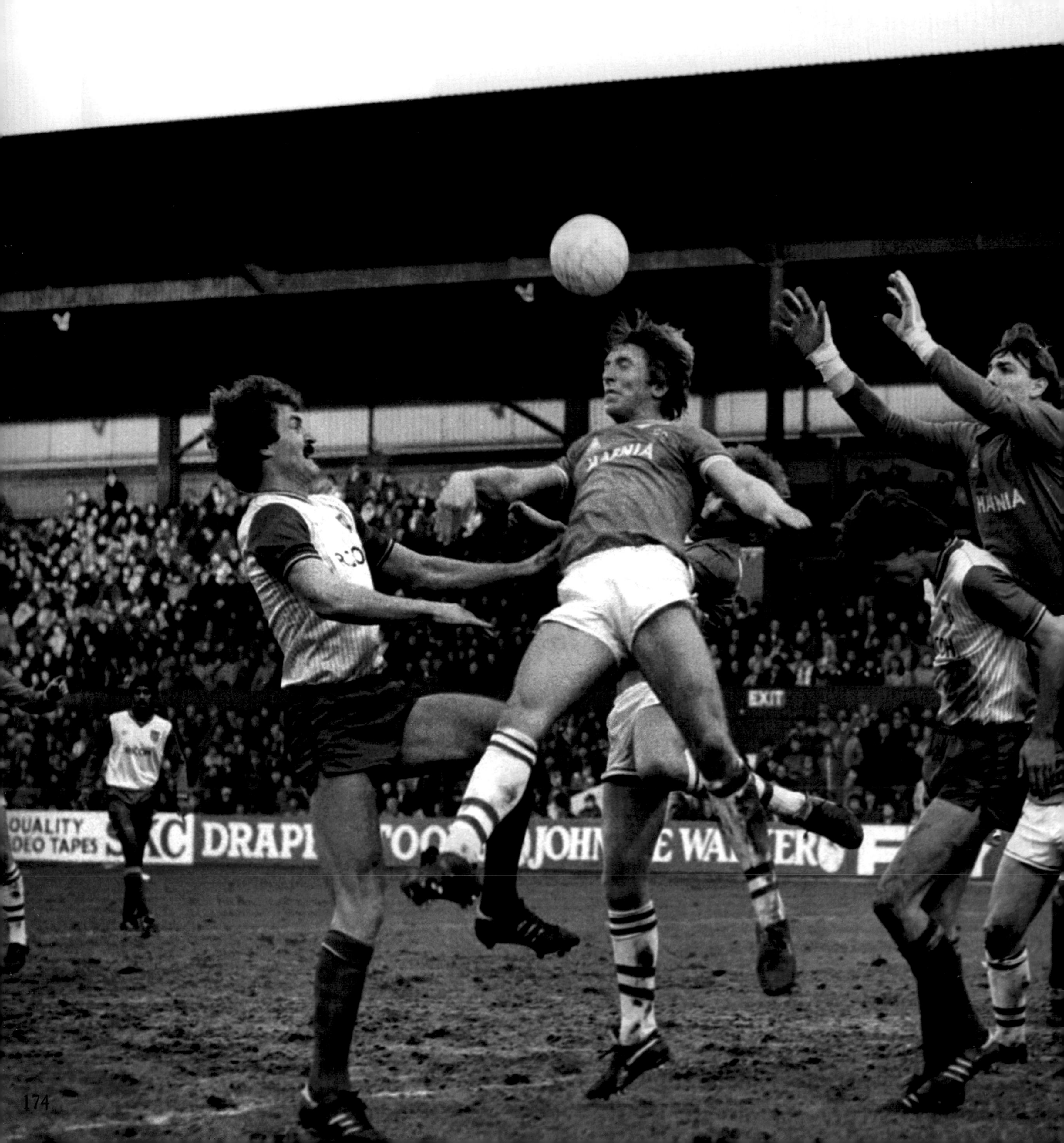
EXIT

ABOVE: England Under-21 striker Adrian Heath signs for Everton, watched by Howard Kendall, in January 1982.

Kendall was certainly well versed in the club's traditions, for he had played a key part in the "School of Science". Howard was coming to the end of an illustrious career and even rejoined Everton as player-manager. In the event, he would hang up his boots after just four more games in the Everton blue in order to concentrate full-time on the job at hand.

Other fresh faces were brought in, including Alan Ainscow, Jim Arnold, Mick Ferguson, Mike Walsh, Neville Southall and Mickey Thomas, or, along with Heath, the "Magnificent Seven" as they were known around Goodison, prior to the start of the 1981–82 season. Perhaps only Southall would go on to make a telling contribution, but all seven contributed to help Everton reach eighth position at the end of the season – a considerable improvement on the previous term.

LEFT: Neville Southall comes out to claim a high ball in an FA Cup tie against Stoke, January 1984.

Trevor Francis surrounded by Everton players Paul Power, Mark Higgins and Billy Wright during a heated exchange that saw Francis sent off, March 1982.

The steady progress continued, with a final league placing of seventh achieved in 1982–83. But the 1983–84 season started dismally and appeared to be getting worse as the months passed. By January the club had won just six of their 21 league matches and were languishing well down the table. The poor performances affected attendances, with just 13,659 bothering to turn out to see a tepid goalless draw against Coventry City, and those that were present made their feelings known throughout much of the match – "Kendall Out!" was the cry.

Fortunately the Board held firm and continued to give him their backing. It is often claimed that Everton's season, indeed their entire history during the decade, changed the moment Adrian Heath scored a late equalizer at Oxford United to earn a replay in the League Cup fifth round. That may well have been true, although the Board have never stated whether or not they were close to calling time on Kendall's tenure.

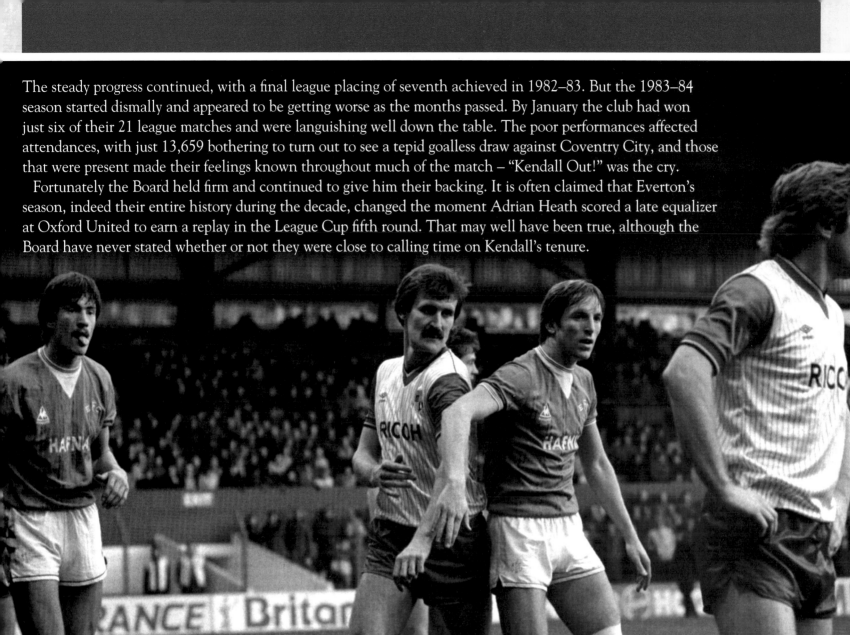

Derek Mountfield and Gary Stevens defend the Everton goal against Stoke in the FA Cup third round, January 1984. Little did they then know, as the team struggled for form, that they would be going all the way to the final.

"
Bring back attractive, winning football. Kendall out!

A banner at Goodison in December 1983
"

Much of the credit for the turnaround in fortunes must also lie with the fact that the players, including new recruits Andy Gray – a £250,000 bargain after his £1.5 million move a few years previously – Peter Reid and Trevor Steven, started to gel. Aston Villa were seen off over two legs to earn Everton a place in the League Cup final for only the second time in their history, where they would face holders Liverpool.

After more than 90 years of history, this was to be the first major Cup final between the two sides, with Liverpool winning 1-0 in a replay to collect the League Cup for the fourth time in succession.

LEFT: Kendall leads his side out alongside his Liverpool counterpart Joe Fagan in 1984.

BELOW: Kevin Sheedy in action for Everton in the 1984 League Cup final. This cultured midfielder with a sweet left foot spent four years in Liverpool's reserves, playing just three first-team games, before a tribunal-fixed £100,000 fee bought his release. His 10 years of service before moving on to Newcastle in 1992 were invaluable, and brought them 45 international caps for Ireland.

In the two previous years, the team the Reds had beaten in the League Cup final had gone on to win the FA Cup the same season, and Everton were handily placed to make further progress in that competition too. They made it back to Wembley where they would face Graham Taylor's Watford side. Although not a classic match, goals either side of half-time from Graeme Sharp and Andy Gray ensured Everton collected their first major trophy for 14 years and returned to European competition the following season.

RIGHT: Andy Gray is congratulated after scoring his controversial goal for Everton in the 1984 FA Cup final. Many believed his challenge on opposing keeper Steve Sherwood was illegal, but the goal stood and a 2-0 win resulted.

Everton captain Kevin Ratcliffe receives the trophy from the Duchess of Kent after his side's victory over Watford at Wembley, May 1984.

LEFT: Everton enjoy their return to Liverpool on an open-top bus with the FA Cup, following their win over Watford. It was 18 long years since their last Wembley triumph against Sheffield Wednesday, and all the more savoured for that reason.

BELOW: Any win over their local rivals was to be celebrated, and Everton did just that after being crowned Charity Shield Winners at Wembley, August 1984. To make it all the sweeter, the single goal was an own goal by Bruce Grobbelaar.

With Neville Southall in particular in majestic form throughout the season, Everton looked like a side that could mount a serious challenge for the title in 1984–85. After a stuttering start the side began to hit top form, especially on their travels, and were there or thereabouts for much of the campaign. Their chief rivals for the title were Tottenham Hotspur, but a 2-1 win at White Hart Lane, where Southall pulled off two world-class saves to guarantee all three points, saw off the Londoners' challenge. The title was won with victory over QPR on 6th May. Everton would finish the season with 90 points, a good 13 ahead of the runners-up.

While in pursuit of the league title, Everton also made progress in the FA Cup and European Cup Winners' Cup, and it looked at one point as though Everton might lift a treble come the end of the season. The Cup Winners' Cup was won 3-1 against Rapid Vienna at Feyenoord's ground, but the key tie had been the clash with Bayern Munich in the semi-final, with Everton drawing 0-0 in Munich and recovering from going a goal down at home to win 3-1.

Merseyside-born Peter Reid was bought for £600,000 from Bolton in 1982. Though dogged by injury during spells of his Goodison tenure, illustrated by less than 200 appearances in seven years, the impact of a fully fit Reid could not be underestimated – particularly in the 1984–85 season where he helped Everton to secure its eighth league title and the European Cup Winners' Cup, winning the PFA Player of the Year gong in the process.

Victory in Europe … Andy Gray celebrates in Rotterdam
alongside Graeme Sharp, Peter Reid and Paul Bracewell.

Three days after the trophy was lifted in Rotterdam, Everton strode out at Wembley to face Manchester United. Although United defender Kevin Moran became the first player to be sent off in an FA Cup final, tiredness killed off Everton long before Norman Whiteside – ironically a future Toffee – scored the only goal of the game.

The Everton and Manchester United teams walk out on to the pitch before the FA Cup final in May 1985. Sadly Everton could not repeat the previous year's performance nor clinch the Double.

In the league there were to be no such disappointments. With the momentum in their favour, Everton powered towards the title, seeing off Arsenal in March with a 2-0 win.

Talent to spare. Left to right (from second left): Paul Bracewell, Adrian Heath, Graeme Sharpe, Peter Reid and Andy Gray.

Champions

ABOVE: Neville Southall and Kevin Ratcliffe applaud fans after Everton win the League Championship, May 1985.

RIGHT: A superb 10-game winning streak between March and early May made sure of the triumph.

The final trophy haul was impressive, the performances more so. Indeed, in Europe in particular Everton had caused many to sit up and take notice and several pundits saw in Everton a side with the potential to fare well in the upcoming European Cup campaign of 1985–86.

Unfortunately, they were never to get the chance: what had been a depressing season as far as crowd trouble and disasters was concerned, with Millwall fans rioting at Luton during an FA Cup tie and 59 people losing their lives in the Bradford fire, reached its nadir during the European Cup final of 1985.

Two days after the Heysel disaster the European governing body imposed their own, indefinite ban, with Liverpool subject to a further three-year ban whenever the blanket ban was lifted.

Everton did what any self-respecting side of the era did and headed into the studio to record an FA Cup final record. At Abbey Road, once the home of The Beatles, in April 1985 are Ian Atkins, Gary Stevens, Adrian Heath, Peter Reid, Alan Harper, Paul Bracewell, Andy Gray, Kevin Richardson and Trevor Steven.

Another Cup final, another Everton record, this time in 1986.

Meanwhile, back at Goodison, even a local nun was getting in on the football act.

—LEGENDS—

Neville Southall

Welsh shot-stopper Neville Southall, known affectionately during his time at Goodison as "Big Nev", was a mainstay at the club for nearly two decades. In his later career he would be known as the oldest player to grace the Premier League, turning out for Bradford City at the grand old age of 41. The achievement was typical of Southall's commitment to the game.

After rejection at Crewe Alexandra and Bolton Wanderers, Neville settled at Bury and caught the eye of Howard Kendall after just one season. Kendall saw enough to bring him to Goodison in 1981 for a fee of £150,000 to challenge then first choice Jim Arnold. A shaky start saw him loaned out to Port Vale in 1983 but he soon returned and usurped Arnold, going on to amass an impressive haul of silverware, including two league titles, a pair of FA Cups, four Charity Shields and a European Cup Winners' Cup during his 18-year stay.

Southall left Everton in 1998 for a brief spell at Stoke before heading to Torquay. He had spells as goalkeeper cover at Rhyl, Shrewsbury, Dover Athletic and Dagenham before hanging up his gloves in 2002 at the age of 43. A spell in caretaker charge of Wales in 1999 prepared Southall for non-league management posts at Dover Athletic and Hastings United, but he would always be best known for his mammoth stint in-between the sticks for Everton.

Big Nev in commanding action.

Name: Neville Southall

Born: Llandudno, 1958

Position: Goalkeeper

Everton Playing Career: 1981–98

Club Appearances: 578

Goals: 0

International Appearances: 92

Goals: 0

Feeling the pressure as Everton slumped to an opening day 4-1 defeat to Spurs. Yet within nine months Neville and his team were champions.

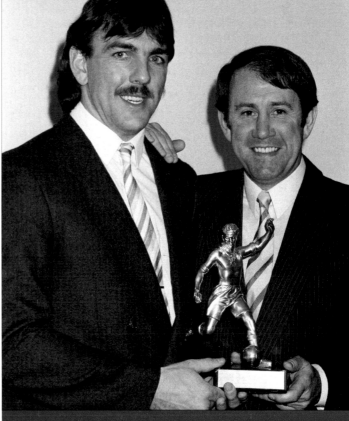

The deserved Footballer of the Year, as decided by the Professional Sportswriters Association, receives his honour from his manager in 1985.

Despite a half-hearted attempt by some of the clubs who had qualified for European competition to pursue legal avenues in an attempt to gain readmittance, the 1985–86 season kicked off with English clubs excluded and marginalized. A short-lived attempt to compensate the six sides denied European football saw the introduction of the Screen Sports Super Cup, with two mini leagues, two semi-finals and a final, but such was the lack of interest even the final was held over to the following season (Liverpool beat Everton over two legs 7-2, although Everton fielded a below-strength side in both games).

The real action was to be found in the race for domestic honours, with Everton and Liverpool leading the chase in both the FA Cup and league. Everton had been strengthened by the arrival of striker Gary Lineker from Leicester City.

A league haul of 30 goals in 41 appearances, coupled with eight cup goals, prevented Lineker from being seen as the villain of the piece for ousting Andy Gray, especially as it was his goals that enabled Everton to top the table for much of the season. Indeed, come April both Everton and Liverpool stood a chance of completing the Double. But disappointing Everton results against Nottingham Forest and Oxford United enabled their neighbours to pip them to the title by two points.

A week after the league was decided, Everton played their part in the first ever all-Merseyside FA Cup final at Wembley. Sadly the game ended in 3-1 defeat.

I'm rather a boring sort of person.

Gary Lineker, on *Desert Island Discs*

ABOVE: Everton manager Howard Kendall with new striker Gary Lineker at Goodison Park in June 1985. Everton beat off competition for the £1 million-rated player from their local rivals and Lineker enjoyed a superb single season in blue.

BELOW: Substitute Alan Harper celebrates after scoring in the 2-1 FA Cup semi-final win over Sheffield Wednesday in 1986.

Lineker beats Bruce Grobbelaar to score Everton's goal in the 1986 FA Cup final, Everton's third in succession. Lineker would soon be on the move after playing for England at the World Cup, attracting a £2.8 million bid from Barcelona.

The disappointment of losing both major trophies to their biggest rivals can only be imagined, but the situation was made worse by the decision, made several weeks earlier, that there would be a combined open-top bus tour the day after the final! Only Peter Reid failed to show up, for which he was fined by Howard Kendall, but no doubt the rest of the Everton team would gladly have put their hands in their pockets rather than suffer this ignominy. The teams did, however, share the Charity Shield.

If anything, the experience of losing the Merseyside Cup final made the Everton players more committed to avoiding a repeat in the future. Once again there were changes to the team. While the new arrivals weren't exactly marquee names, the likes of Dave Watson would become Everton stalwarts for years to come.

With Neville Southall in goal and the likes of Trevor Steven, Gary Stevens, Derek Mountfield, Peter Reid, Kevin Ratcliffe and Kevin Sheedy still at the peak of their powers, Everton would mount another strong challenge for the league title in 1986–87. Despite the firepower at their disposal, it was a defender, Pat van den Hauwe (a full Welsh international despite being born in Belgium) who scored the goal that secured the title at Norwich City.

LEFT: Battling midfielder Trevor Steven was the dynamo that powered the Toffees to the title. Here he masterminds a 2-1 victory at Stamford Bridge, April 1987, with ultimate victory just days away.

ABOVE: Manager Howard Kendall celebrates at Carrow Road as his team win the title. He would not be round for much longer, however, as he soon departed for Spanish gold.

RIGHT: Captain Kevin Ratcliffe holds the league trophy aloft, having received it from Bobby Robson after a win against Spurs at Goodison Park.

Everton captain Kevin Ratcliffe (right) and team-mate Dave Watson celebrate winning the title with a glass of champagne in the dressing room at Goodison Park.

FOOTBALL –STATS–
Kevin Ratcliffe

Name: Kevin Ratcliffe

Born: Mancot, 1960

Position: Central defender

Everton Playing Career: 1980–91

Club Appearances: 493

Goals: 2

International Appearances: 59

Goals: 0

–LEGENDS– Kevin Ratcliffe

This combative central defender was a fixture for club and country in front of team-mate Neville Southall for more than a decade, winning 59 international caps for Wales and leading Everton to the League, FA Cup and Cup Winners' Cup, becoming one of the club's most successful captains.

Having spent much of his childhood on the Goodison terraces, Ratcliffe broke through in 1980–81, having previously played two first-team games. He shut out the formidable Joe Jordan on his debut at Old Trafford in 1980. Originally playing at left-back under Gordon Lee, he flourished in his natural central role under Howard Kendall. Luckily a transfer to Ipswich fell through, as he was soon skippering Everton and Wales, becoming in 1984 the youngest man since Bobby Moore, two decades earlier, to hold the FA Cup aloft.

Ratcliffe was not the most skilful of footballers but he anticipated superbly, tackled ferociously and did the simple things well. He was also deceptively fast; even if the Everton offside trap was breached, he was often able to turn and catch the striker. He moved on to Dundee and then Cardiff after being replaced by Martin Keown in 1991, and would manage Chester City and Shrewsbury before opting for a career as a pundit with BBC Wales.

–LEGENDS–

Graeme Sharp

Best remembered for his partnership with Andy Gray, Sharp was paired with Adrian Heath after Gordon Lee paid Dumbarton £120,000 for his services as the Eighties began.

He played in all three Merseyside Wembley finals in that decade but scored in none, though he did score in the win against Watford in 1984. He followed that with the equalizer against Bayern Munich in the Cup Winners' Cup semi-final the following season, and it was 1985 that saw Scotland award him the first of 12 full caps in a World Cup qualifier against Iceland. Despite the attentions of clubs in Italy, Sharp stayed at Goodison and by the time he left in 1991 he had established himself as Everton's top postwar goalscorer.

Sharp forged partnerships with Gary Lineker and Wayne Clarke, the man bought to replace him, and in 424 domestic games he scored 146 goals. Sharp notched 30 in all competitions in 1984–85, his best season.

His move to Oldham aged 30 still saw him command a £500,000 fee, and four years later he became the Lancashire Club's manager as Joe Royle returned to Merseyside to succeed Mike Walker at Goodison.

FOOTBALL –STATS–

Graeme Sharp

Name: Graeme Sharp
Born: Glasgow, 1960
Position: Striker
Everton Playing Career: 1980–91
Club Appearances: 446
Goals: 159
International Appearances: 12
Goals: 1

Graeme Sharp calls for the ball record a 2-1 win at Villa Park, May 1982.

Life Off the Field

On the Birth of your Son

LEFT: Dave Watson and wife welcome their newborn baby in 1986.

RIGHT: Derek Mountfield and Julie Bird tie the knot in 1984 …

FAR RIGHT: … while Howard Kendall manages to avoid getting tied up in any knots with kissogram girl Maureen Jenner wishing him good luck before the 1984 FA Cup final.

If there was one aspect of managing Everton during the 1980s that rankled with Howard Kendall, it was the denial of European competition. Eventually, with there being no immediate prospect of the indefinite ban being lifted, Kendall accepted the opportunity of becoming manager of Athletic Bilbao. Everton did not have far to look for a replacement, promoting first-team coach Colin Harvey to become the second member of the "Holy Trinity" to take the mantle of manager.

Many of the players during the glory run in the Eighties cited Harvey as a chief reason for the club's success and there was great hope that the transition would be seamless. Unfortunately, managing a club would prove to be a different prospect to coaching and, rather than build on their success, Everton began to slip back down the table. While never out of the top 10, final placings of fourth, eighth and sixth were major disappointments after the four seasons of success that had gone before.

The *Daily Mirror* reports on Howard Kendall's departure for sunnier climes.

There was an extended run in the FA Cup in 1989 when Everton would again make it all the way to Wembley where, once again, Liverpool lay in wait. This time the city was united in the aftermath of the Hillsborough tragedy that left 96 people dead. If Liverpool's eventual victory was seen as a fitting memorial to those who had died, Everton deserved credit for their efforts in an open game, which their opponents edged 3-2 after extra-time.

One week after Hillsborough, Everton players and manager bowed their heads (above) in remembrance during a minute's silence at Goodison.

In 1991 in the fifth round of the FA Cup Everton went to Anfield and held Liverpool to a goalless draw. The replay at Goodison was an epic 4-4 draw. A week later Everton won the second replay 1-0, only to lose in the sixth round to West Ham … it was that kind of season.

Everton had started the campaign poorly and were close to the relegation spots by the end of October. The Board sacked Colin Harvey and sent out a call to Howard Kendall, who had by now returned from Spain and taken over at Manchester City. A quick drive down the M62 saw Kendall reinstalled as boss, with Harvey appointed his assistant.

If the hope was that the pair would bring the glory days back, the reality was different, with two successive mid-table finishes.

Kendall and Harvey, two thirds of the "Holy Trinity" as players, pray for a miracle as Aston Villa, guided by Ron Atkinson (behind them), puts one more nail in their managerial coffin.

Despite an encouraging start to 1993–94 Everton soon lost form and sight of the top, prompting Kendall to leave the club in December. His eventual replacement was Mike Walker, whose achievements on a smaller budget at Norwich City, taking them into Europe after the UEFA ban had been lifted, had earned praise. Walker could do little to halt the dangerous slide down the table, however, and there was a real danger that Everton's spell in the top flight was going to come to an end after 40 years.

When Wimbledon visited Goodison Park on the final day of the 1993–94 season, Everton occupied the third relegation spot, a point behind Sheffield United, Ipswich Town and Southampton. Everton soon found themselves two goals behind, the news that the other threatened teams were all drawing only adding to the tension. Somehow Everton found the will to live, scoring through Graham Stuart and Barry Horne to draw level and then, with nine minutes left, taking the lead through Stuart. A nervous close to the game saw Everton hold what they had and secure safety at the expense of Sheffield United, who shipped two late goals at Chelsea.

This brush with relegation should have prompted a revival, but the 1994–95 season seemed to offer more of the same and, with the team firmly rooted to the bottom of the table, the Board sacked Walker. Once again Everton turned to one of their old boys for salvation.

Former centre-forward and Goodison hero Joe Royle's brief was simple: to ensure the club's continued presence in the top flight, which he eventually did thanks to a win against already relegated Ipswich a week before the season ended. There was something of a bonus too, for while the league campaign had been a disaster, the FA Cup offered a welcome distraction that saw the club march all the way to Wembley.

Up against them were Manchester United. Although cast in the role of underdogs, Everton rose to the occasion and scored the only goal of the game through Paul Rideout to win the cup for the fifth time. It was the cup victory that best lived up to the club's motto "Nil Satis Nisi Optimum" – Nothing but the best is good enough.

207

Acknowledgements

The author would like to acknowledge the contributions of Graham Betts and Drew Heatley.

This book is dedicated to the memory of Evertonians David Heatley and Geoff Eccles.

Special thanks to Vito Inglese for his expert picture research and assistance.

Thanks also to Adam Powley and Rebecca Ellis.